THE COMPLETE LIBRARY SKILLS— GRADE 5

By
Linda Turrell

Cover and Inside Illustrations by
Darcy Myers

Publishers
T.S. Denison & Co., Inc.
Minneapolis, Minnesota 55431

Standard Book Number: 513-02212-0
The Complete Library Skills—Grade 5
Copyright © 1994 by T.S. Denison & Co., Inc.
9601 Newton Avenue South
Minneapolis, Minnesota 55431

Printed in the USA

CONTENTS

Welcoming Fifth-Graders To The Library 4
The Card Catalog 5
Title Cards 6
Subject Cards 7
Author Cards 8

Guide Letters 9
Guide Letter Activity 10
Media Cards 11
Media Cards Activities 12-13
Using Catalog Cards & Subjects 14
What Type of Card Do You Need? 15
Name That Catalog Card 16
What Type of Card Do You Choose? 17-18
What Subject Do You Look Under? 19

Dewey Decimal System 20
Dewey Decimal System Activities 21-23
Dewey Call Numbers 24
Dewey Call Numbers Activity 25
Dewey Numbers-Call Numbers 26
Dewey Numbers Activity 27
Name That Dewey Number & Subject 28-29
Overview-The Dewey Decimal System 30

Parts of a Book 31
The Copyright Page 32
Using the Title Page & Copyright Page 33-34
The Table of Contents 35-37
The Index 38-39
The Book Index 40
The Index Page 41
The Book Index Activities 42-44
Comparing Table of Contents & Index 45
Comparing Contents & Index Activities 46-48
The Illustration Page 49
Using the Illustration Page Activities 50
The Glossary 51
The Glossary Activities 52

Magazines 53
Magazine Table of Contents Page 54
The Children's Magazine Guide 55
Children's Magazine Guide Activity 56
Using a Magazine Guide 57
Magazines-Writing to be Published 58
Magazine Market List 59

The Newspaper Index 60
Using a Newspaper Index Activity 61-62

Encyclopedias 63
The Encyclopedia Index 64

Studying the Encyclopedia Index 65
Comparing Encyclopedia Indexes 66-71
Using Headings 72
Subheadings 73
Encyclopedia Headings Activity 74
Subheading Activity 75
Heading & Subheading Activity 76

See Also References 77
See Also References Activities 78-80
Overview-Using The Encyclopedia Index 81
Overview-Comparing Encyclopedias 82
Encyclopedia Investigation 83
Where in the World is it? 84
Comparing Encyclopedia Activities 85-86

Using Specialized Encyclopedias 87
Using the Specialized Encyclopedia 88-89

The Atlas 90
Using an Atlas 91
Mapping 92
Atlas Activity 93
Examining an Atlas 94

The Biographical Dictionary 95
Using the Biographical Dictionary 96
Webster's New Biographical Dictionary 97-99
Specialized Kind of Biographical Dictionary 100

The Junior Book of Authors
Third Junior Book of Authors
Fourth Junior Book of Authors 101
Using Reference Books Review 102

Writing A Book Report 103
Writing a Book Report Activity 104

The Newbery Award 105
Newbery Winners & Honor Books 106-111

The Poem 112
Poetry Devices 113-115
Poetry Devices-Matching 116

Science Fiction? Science Fact? 117
Science Fiction Activities 118-119

Tall Tales 120
Tall Tale Activities 121-122

Suggested Authors for Grade Five 123
The Glossary 124-126

WELCOMING FIFTH-GRADERS TO THE LIBRARY

By the time children reach fifth grade they are ready and eager to use all the components of the library. They are capable of searching the shelves for fiction and nonfiction books; they enjoy discovering and examining reference materials; and, are able to use a variety of multimedia materials.

The Complete Library Skills — Grade Five presents an excellent overview of the card catalog, with emphasis on how one chooses the appropriate card (author, title, subject) and how to locate these cards. From this review the children complete a study of the Dewey Decimal System, ranging from how books are categorized in the system, to how books are organized by Dewey call numbers.

The parts of a book section covers topics such as, how children can locate information in a book; use an index, copyright page, table of contents, illustration pages, and glossary, and how to evaluate whether the information in the book they have chosen could be of use in writing a report.

Researching with magazines, *The Children's Magazine Guide*, the newspaper, encyclopedias, specialized encyclopedias, the atlas, biographical dictionary, and the *Junior Book of Authors* are all presented in detail. These are reference materials that fifth grade students will be able to effectively use for topic reports and for searching out information of interest.

The final literature section of *The Complete Library Skills — Grade Five,* introduces the children to the Newbery Winners and the Newbery Honor Books, as well as poetry, science fiction, and tall tales.

At the end of the fifth grade year, these capable ten and eleven-year-old children will be able to use the library with skill and confidence, and delight in the wealth of knowledge and information provided for them in their library!

THE CARD CATALOG

The card catalog is a collection of author, title, and subject cards grouped together. It is a guide for you. Think of it as a giant telephone book for the books in the library. Each of the three cards gives the same information. The only item that is different is the first line of each card. The author card begins with the last name of the author, the title card begins with the title of the book, and the subject card begins with the subject of the book. Subject cards are written in all capital letters.

These cards give you the address where the book can be found in the library. You know how to use the telephone book to find an address or phone number. Think of the card catalog working in the same way. If you need to find information go to the card catalog and decide in which section you need to look. Do you know the title of your book? If you do, choose the title section. Do you know the author's name? If you do, choose the author section. Do you know what your book is about but do not know the book title or author's name? Choose the subject section.

Now look at the first word of the title. Remember not to count the words *a*, *an*, and *the*. Your book will be under that first word. For example: *The Shady Tree* will be found under S.

What if you only know that *The Shady Tree* written by Peter Leaf, is about a mystery that takes place in the country. You go to the subject section and look under MYSTERY because that is the subject of the book.

What if you want a book by Peter Leaf but can't remember the title? Go to the author section and look under *Leaf*.

TITLE CARDS

Fic Fe	The Mystery of the Green Parrot Feather, Sally Mystery of the green parrot. Trenton: New Jersey. Pellet Press, 1988. 63 p. illus. This is the story of a parrot and his adventures in his strange cage. 1. Fiction—Parrot stories I. Title

1. _____   What is the title of this book?

2. _____   Who is the author?

3. _____   What year was the book published?

4. _____   What is the call number?

5. _____   What is the book about?

6. _____   How many pages are in the book?

7. _____   Who published it?

8. _____   Where was it published?

9. _____   Is it a fiction book?

10. _____   What is the subject heading?

SUBJECT CARD

599
Nu

SQUIRRELS

Nutt, Jeremy

The truth about squirrels. Tree, New Jersey.

Tree Press, 1988.

This book tells the facts and fiction about squirrels.
Illustrations are large and describe their homes.

1. _____ What is the title of this book?

2. _____ Who is the author?

3. _____ What year was the book published?

4. _____ What is the call number?

5. _____ What is the book about?

6. _____ How many pages are in the book?

7. _____ Who published it?

8. _____ Where was it published?

9. _____ Is it a fiction book?

10. _____ What is the subject heading?

AUTHOR CARD

599
Nu

Nutt, Jeremy

The truth about squirrels. Tree, New Jersey.

Tree Press, 1988.

111 p. illus.

This book tells the facts and fiction about squirrels.
Illustrations are large and describe their homes.

1. _____   What is the title of this book?

2. _____   Who is the author?

3. _____   What year was the book published?

4. _____   What is the call number?

5. _____   What is the book about?

6. _____   How many pages are in the book?

7. _____   Who published it?

8. _____   Where was it published?

9. _____   Is it a fiction book?

10. _____   What is the subject heading?

GUIDE LETTERS

The card catalog has letters on each box drawer. They are in alphabetical order. They tell you what cards are in each drawer. For example, a drawer marked A–D will have cards beginning with A, B, C, and D.

Remember the card catalog is divided into three parts. The subject, author and title sections are labelled. If you are looking for a title card in the card catalog, it will have the word "title" on each drawer in the section. The guide letters will be under this word.

For example, say you are looking at the very first drawer in the catalog box. What do you see? The word "author" and the letters A–D.

```
┌─────────────────────────┐
│                         │
│         Author          │
│                         │
│          A–D            │
│                         │
└─────────────────────────┘
```

If you want to find a book written by Alice A. Apple, would you find it in this drawer? Yes, you would. What if you were looking for a book with the title *An Apple for Alice*? Would it be in this drawer? No, it would not. Titles are in the next section of the box. You will not find titles in the author section. And you will not find subjects in the author section.

What if you were looking for a book about the uses of apples? Would you look in the title, author, or subject section of the card catalog? You would look in the subject section. Good. Under what letter would you look? "A" would be the letter because your subject is apples.

The drawer would look like this:

```
┌─────────────────────────┐
│                         │
│         Subject         │
│                         │
│          A–D            │
│                         │
└─────────────────────────┘
```

This type of catalog is called a divided catalog. It is in three parts or sections and it is quick and easy to use. But not all catalogs are arranged in this manner. Some libraries have card catalogs which have all the cards in alphabetical order. The title, author, and subject cards are mixed. Some library users prefer this method.

Remember that the card catalog is like a book of introductions. Each card tells you a bit about the book. Keep this in mind when you use the guide letters. They are there to guide you to the information you need.

GUIDE LETTERS

author A–E	title A–D	subject A– C
author F–H	title E–K	subject D–H
author I–M	title L–R	subject I–M
author N–R	title S–T	subject N–R
author S–Z	title U–Z	subject S–Z

Name the drawer you would use to find information on the situations. Remember: You must first choose a title, author, or subject.

1. *Spiders* _____

2. *The Complete Book of Spiders* _____

3. *Mark Twain* _____

4. *Dinosaurs* _____

5. *Baseball* _____

6. *The Green Gerbil* _____

7. *Space* _____

8. *Learning about the Stars* _____

9. *The Story of the Lady Bug* _____

10. *Stars* _____

MEDIA CARDS

Media cards work in the same way subject, title, and author cards work in the card catalog. They tell you where you can find specific types of information. Media cards tell you if your library has cassette tapes, a picture file, a vertical file, slides, or filmstrips.

These sources of information are not books. You know what a cassette, and filmstrips are, but you may be unfamiliar with a vertical file, picture file, and slides.

The vertical file is a collection of small items such as newspaper clippings, magazine clippings, pamphlets (small papers), charts, or posters. It can be anything that gives a bit of information in a small space. Vertical files can be helpful to you when you are writing a report. Let's say that you are writing about the nesting habits of the ant. Go to the vertical file. The vertical file is arranged in different ways in different libraries. But many libraries like to use the Dewey Decimal System. Ants would be in the science section, the 500s.

Pull the file. Let's say that a teacher has cut an old magazine article from a discarded magazine. The article is called "Ants Build Their Homes."

Let's say that you would like a large picture for the cover of your report. Go to the picture file. Look under animals—insects. Let's say that you find a large picture of the ant. It is just what you need.

Will you show any slides for your report? Does your library have any slides? Let's find out. Go to the card catalog. Look under ants. Do you see any specially marked cards? Let's say, you do. Under ants find three cards. They are called: "The Ants," "Ants and Their Homes," and "Types of Ants Found Throughout the World." Can you use any of these slides? Yes, you can use the first two slides. The third one does not really go with your subject.

If you look at the card catalog, how can you tell quickly that your library has these information sources? Usually libraries color code these cards. That is, they use a color to tell the library user what form the information is in. For example, records may have a blue line on the top of the card. In this way you know immediately that the information on the card can be found in the form of a record. Red may mean that the information is in the vertical file. Yellow may mean the information is in cassette form. The colors vary from library to library. But the color for each type of information is the same within each library.

Let's look at some media cards and learn how to use them.

MEDIA CARDS

In this library you can find media cards for the following.

cassette tapes	yellow
pictures	green
records	blue
slides	orange
filmstrips	purple
vertical file	red

Read the following situations. What type of card will give you the information you need? Write the type of media card and its color.

1. _____ Where will you find a song about the presidents on a 33 r.p.m. record?

2. _____ You need a picture for your report about Sir Francis Drake?

3. _____ Your teacher plans a filmstrip about the early explorers. Does the library have one?

4. _____ Your teacher plans to play a cassette tape of *The Story of Peter Rabbit.* Does the library have it?

5. _____ You need a picture of a dinosaur. Where do you go?

6. _____ You plan to include a map of Columbus' trip to the New World. Where do you go?

7. _____ You plan to show a slide of Spain for your report. Where do you go?

8. _____ You need a short article about good nutrition. Where do you go?

9. _____ You need to know what the first illustration of Santa Claus looked like in order to draw a picture for your report about holidays. Where do you go?

10. _____ You need a picture of the blue jay for your report about birds. Where do you go?

MEDIA CARDS

In this library you can find media cards for the following.

cassette tapes	yellow
pictures	green
records	blue
slides	orange
filmstrips	purple
vertical file	red

Read the following situations. What type of card will give you the information you need? Write the type of media card and its color.

1. _____ Your history teacher showed a film about volcanoes. You plan an extra credit report about volcanoes. Where do you look for color pictures of Mt. Saint Helens, the volcano?

2. _____ Your school is celebrating its twenty-fifth anniversary. Are there any records on file that show how old the school looked twenty-five years ago? Where do you look?

3. _____ Your teacher loves birds. She plans an entire unit on birds including birds' songs. Can you find songs of the most common birds? Where do you look?

4. _____ To add to your teacher's unit on birds, you plan to show pictures of the most common birds. Where do you go?

5. _____ The poster contest theme is "Sport Safety." Is there a filmstrip your teacher can show about this subject? Where do you look?

6. _____ Your class plans a story hour for the younger grades. You plan to tell a fairy tale. But you need music with your story. What media cards do you check?

7. _____
_____ Does the library have a copy of *Peter Rabbit*? You need to play a copy of it for the younger classes. What two media cards do you check?

8. _____ You love cars. Your project for the history fair will be the "History of the American Car." Where can you find what the first American car looked like? Name the media card.

USING CATALOG CARDS
AND SUBJECTS

It helps you if you know how to find what you need in the card catalog. Often, you will have an idea of what you need but you don't know exactly how to find it. This situation happens often, especially when you are using the subject part of the card catalog.

You may know that you need information about sports. You need to find the rules of baseball. Where do you look? You could look under sports. Sports is a large subject heading. You might have to read through several cards to find what you need. You could look under baseball. This narrows your search. You may need to look through less catalog cards. Now check the cards on baseball. Read the book descriptions. Is there any mention about the rules of baseball? If so, your search is complete. Let's try another example. You are planning a report about treasure ships and the explorers. Where do you look? You could look under ships. But that is a large subject. You could look under treasure ships. That does narrow your subject. Or you could look under explorers. Again, that is a general subject. But you do need information about the explorers. So your best choices would be explorers and treasure ships.

When using the subject section of the card catalog, remember to think about the type of information that you need.

The Card Catalog — Name That Subject

1. _____ You want a book about dogs. But you only need to find information about how to care for them. Name that subject.

2. _____ You think hockey is great! You plan a game after school but you are uncertain of the rules. Name that subject.

3. _____ You need to find a good book for your younger brother. You are thinking about a cute story about mice. Name that subject.

4. _____ The Plains Indians is the subject of your next report. You plan to write about the games their children play. Name that subject.

5. _____ You plan to make your own holiday cards this year. Where do you look?

WHAT TYPE OF CARD DO YOU NEED?

Often you may stand before the card catalog and wonder what kind of card do I really need? The card you will choose depends upon the type of information you have. Let's say that you are looking for a book about rock collecting. You need it for a school project. You do not know the author's name. You do not know the title of the book. But you do know the subject: rock collecting. You may check under the subject rocks and or rock collection.

What if you know the title of the book? Check under the title section. And if you know the author's name? Check under the author section. Let's say your teacher needs to know if there are enough books in the library for a future assignment. Your class is going to write reports about mystery books. Does the library have twenty-five mystery books? How do you find out? Do you look under the author's name? No. Under the title? No. Under the subject section? Yes. You may look under the subject; mystery.

Let's look at some catalog card situations.

NAME THAT CATALOG CARD

Read each sentence below. Decide what type catalog card will help you. Remember you may choose a subject card, author card, or title card.

Write subject, author, or title for each sentence.

1. _____ Can you find seven mystery books in your library?

2. _____ Does the library have all the books by Jay T. Book?

3. _____ Who wrote *The Mystery of the Green Parrot*?

4. _____ Can you find the illustrator who drew the pictures for *The Green Caterpillar*?

5. _____ Does the library have twenty-four books, one for each student in your class on craft projects?

6. _____ You adore horses. Does the library have any books about horses?

7. _____ Did Sally Q. Bookmark write twelve or twenty-four books?

8. _____ How many illustrations are in *The Purple Shoe Mystery*?

9. _____ Does the library have any ghost stories?

10. _____ Can you find three books about the same country in the library? The country is Spain.

11. _____ How many chapters are in the book *All About Stars*?

12. _____ Is there only one book about spiders in the library?

13. _____ Was *Happy Moon* written in 1988?

14. _____ Did Greenpond Press publish the book, *Green Frogs*?

15. _____ *Happy Faces* is about good friends. True or false?

WHAT TYPE CATALOG CARD
DO YOU CHOOSE?

Read the sentences below. In each situation you will find the information more quickly if you use the card catalog. Which card would you choose? Author, subject, or title?

1. _____ You need a book about insects for your report. Does the library have any books about insects?

2. _____ Beverly Cleary has written how many books?

3. _____ Who wrote *The Purple Grasshopper*?

4. _____ Did Henry Buggins write a book about dinosaurs?

5. _____ Is *Benjamin Bunny* one of Beatrix Potter's books?

6. _____ Is *The Case of the Yellow Banana* one of several books written by Arthur Spyglass?

7. _____ What books about famous people can you find in the biography section of your library?

8. _____ Your class plans to write reports about the states. How many books about the states does your library have?

9. _____ Are there any books about Samuel Clemens in your library?

10. _____ Is coral really a sea animal or a plant?

11. _____ You must read a mystery. Are there any such books in your library?

12. _____ You heard that *The Orange Who Wore Tennis Shoes* is a funny book. Who is the author?

13. _____ Does the library have any books about how to make craft projects?

14. _____ Where can you find a book about learning French?

15. _____ Does the library have a book about the solar system written by Susan Starlight?

16. _____ You plan to write an extra credit report about a president, George Washington. Where do you look?

NAME _____

WHAT TYPE CARD DO YOU USE?

Read the sentences below. In each situation you will find the information more quickly if you use the card catalog. Which card do you choose? Author, subject, or title?

1. _____ Does the library have any books about volcanoes?

2. _____ Does the library have *Ladybug, Ladybug* by James Peterson?

3. _____ How many books in the library are written by Samuel Clemens?

4. _____ Is *The Mystery of the Purple Shoe* one of a series of mystery books?

5. _____ You need a biography of a famous person for a report. What type card do you need?

6. _____ How many books about dinosaurs are in the library?

7. _____ Does the library have a book about insects written by Peter J. Bug?

8. _____ Are there any books about drawing in the library?

9. _____ Does the library have any books about cooking written by Joan Cook?

10. _____ Can you find any books about sports in the library?

WHAT SUBJECT DO YOU LOOK UNDER?

Read each research situation. What subjects do you check to find the information that you need?

1. Is the ladybug a harmful insect? Check _____ and then

   _____.

2. You are writing a report about the planets. You need a picture of where the

   planets are in the solar system. What two subjects do you look under?

   _____ and _____.

3. You are writing a report about coral and other sea animals. What general

   subject do you check first? _____. What second subject do

   you check? _____.

4. Your science teacher plans to demonstrate how magnets work. This is just

   the first in a series of science experiments planned for this chapter. You

   plant to conduct a science experiment for the class, too. What subject do you

   check? _____.

5. Your cousin plans to visit. He is a baseball fan. Where do you find all the

   official rules before the big game? _____.

DEWEY DECIMAL SYSTEM— CALL NUMBERS

The Dewey Decimal System is a method of putting books in order on the library shelves. Melvil Dewey created this system for nonfiction books. There are ten divisions. Each division is divided again and once again. Each division holds books about the same subject. Let's look at the system.

000–099	**General Works**—dictionaries and encyclopedias
100–199	**Philosophy**—ideas of mankind
200–299	**Religion**
300–399	**Social Sciences**—laws, government, fairy tales, folk tales
400–499	**Languages**
500–599	**Sciences**—rocks, animals, insects
600–699	**Useful Arts**—(how things work) cooking, pet care, how roads are made
700–799	**Arts**—painting, photography, arts and crafts, sports, music, drawing
800–899	**Literature**—poems, plays, short stories
900–999	**Geography and History**—history, travel, biography, atlases

000–099	**General Works**—This division is really a reference division. You will find dictionaries and encyclopedias in this section.
100–199	**Philosophy**—This division contains the basic ideas that mankind has written. Do not be concerned with this division. You most likely will not be using it.
200–299	**Religion**—This division holds all the ideas of the religions of the world.
300–399	**Social Sciences**—This division holds books about the laws, governments, or literature of countries. If you need a book about how laws are made, see the 300s. If you need to know how the government works, see 300s. If you need to know about the customs of a country, see 300s. And if you are interested in folk tales (stories of a certain country) see the 300s.
400–499	**Languages**—This division holds books about foreign languages. If you want to learn French, Spanish, or any other language, see the 400s.
500–599	**Sciences**—If you need a book about insects, or rocks, or animals, or anything that falls into the science area, see the 500s.
600–699	**Useful Arts**—If you need to know how something works, see the 600s. Hobbies, such as cooking or pet care, are in this division.
700–799	**Arts**—Anything in the arts belongs in the 700s. Sports, music, any arts and crafts, painting, and drawing are in here.
800–899	**Literature**—Stories, plays, and poems are in here.
900–999	**Geography and History**—Books about history, travel, and geography (atlases) are in here.

It is not necessary to memorize or learn each division of the Dewey Decimal System. If you want to use the library more effectively be aware of the ten divisions and how they work. Most libraries will have a chart of the Dewey Decimal System. You can check the chart.

NAME _____

DEWEY DECIMAL SYSTEM

000–099	General Reference	Dictionaries, encyclopedias
100–199	Philosophy	Ideas of mankind
200–299	Religion	
300–399	Social Science	Government, how laws are made, fairy tales of all parts of the world
400–499	Languages	
500–599	Science	Animals, planets, space, rocks
600–699	Useful Arts	Cooking, pet care, transportation
700–799	Fine Arts	Art, music, sports, crafts
800–899	Literature	Plays, short stories, poems, novels
900–999	Geography and History	Atlases, travel, biography, history

Read the following book titles. Under what Dewey category would you find them? Under what Dewey number would you find them?

1. _____ *The Care of Mice*

2. _____ *Pet Care: Guinea Pigs*

3. _____ *Football: What are the Rules?*

4. _____ *How to Learn Spanish*

5. _____ *The Way Our Laws are Made*

6. _____ *Rocks and Minerals*

7. _____ *Let's Learn About Spiders*

8. _____ *Baseball*

9. _____ *How to Make Puppets*

10. _____ *Seashells*

11. _____ *How an Indian Makes His Home*

12. _____ *Poems of the Indians*

13. _____ *New Jersey: Its History*

14. _____ *Coral: Fun Facts*

15. _____ *What Makes Leaves Green?*

16. _____ *All About Venus*

17. _____ *Learning to Play the Flute*

18. _____ *The Atlas of the World*

19. _____ *The Children's Dictionary*

NAME _____

DEWEY DECIMAL SYSTEM

000–099	General Reference	Dictionaries, encyclopedias
100–199	Philosophy	Ideas of mankind
200–299	Religion	
300–399	Social Science	Government, how laws are made, fairy tales of all parts of the world
400–499	Languages	
500–599	Science	Animals, planets, space, rocks
600–699	Useful Arts	Cooking, pet care, transportation
700–799	Fine Arts	Art, music, sports, crafts
800–899	Literature	Plays, short stories, poems, novels
900–999	Geography and History	Atlases, travel, biography, history

Read the following book titles. Under what Dewey subject would you find them? Under what Dewey number would you find them.

1. _____ *Rodents and Rabbits*

2. _____ *Pet Care: Gerbils*

3. _____ *How to Learn German*

4. _____ *Karate: The Useful Sport*

5. _____ *The Way the Constitution Works*

6. _____ *Trees of North America*

7. _____ *Let's Learn About Sharks*

8. _____ *Soccer*

9. _____ *How to Work with Clay*

10. _____ *Cooking for Beginners*

11. _____ *Poems for Young People*

12. _____ *The History of the American Revolution*

13. _____ *The Geography of India*

14. _____ *Let's Learn French*

15. _____ *Learn to Play the Piano*

16. _____ *Spooky Stories*

17. _____ *Insects*

18. _____ *Space: Let's Learn About It*

DEWEY DECIMAL SYSTEM

000–099	General Reference	Dictionaries, encyclopedias
100–199	Philosophy	Ideas of mankind
200–299	Religion	
300–399	Social Science	Government, how laws are made, fairy tales of all parts of the world
400–499	Languages	
500–599	Science	Animals, planets, space, rocks
600–699	Useful Arts	Cooking, pet care, transportation
700–799	Fine Arts	Art, music, sports, crafts
800–899	Literature	Plays, short stories, poems, novels
900–999	Geography and History	Atlases, travel, biography, history

Read the following book titles, subjects, or situations. Can you decide what Dewey number and subject will help you?

1. _____ A biography of Paul Revere

2. _____ A book of maps

3. _____ How to make jewelry

4. _____ "The Little Tree" (a poem)

5. _____ How to play chess

6. _____ The building of roads in the U.S.A.

7. _____ The fairy tale of *Jack and the Beanstalk*

8. _____ How a law is made in the U.S.A.

9. _____ Visiting Maine

10. _____ Cooking for beginners

11. _____ Learning about starfish

12. _____ How to make paper crafts for the holidays

13. _____ Learning how bridges are made

14. _____ Drawing horses

15. _____ A French dictionary

DEWEY CALL NUMBERS

A call number located on the spine of the book tells you where you can find that book in the library. The number tells you what section of the library holds the book and the letters come from the first two letters of the author's last name.

Example: All About Insects by Jay T. Bugg has a call number of;

> 595
> Bu

Sometimes call numbers will have a decimal point.

Example: 595.1 This is just a way of dividing the sections in the system again.

Call numbers are arranged in number order. Then the numbers following the point are put in order. And then the letters of the author's name are put in order.

Example: 92.1
92.5   Which comes first? 92.1

Example: 974.1
975.1   Which comes first? 974.1

Example: 92.1
Ab

92.1
Tr   Which comes first? 92.1
                              Ab

DEWEY CALL NUMBERS

Put these Dewey call numbers in order.

910.2	1. _____	791.1 Bl	1. _____
796	2. _____	643.1 Ar	2. _____
398.2	3. _____	643.1 Am	3. _____
920	4. _____	643.3 Br	4. _____
581	5. _____	654.2 Tr	5. _____
921	6. _____	791.2 Br	6. _____
468.3	7. _____	768.5 Br	7. _____
599	8. _____	398.2 Ta	8. _____
641	9. _____	398.2 Tr	9. _____
636	10. _____	398.2 Tn	10. _____

300	1. _____	791.2 Ba	1. _____
009.1	2. _____	791.1 Bl	2. _____
220.5	3. _____	643.1 Ar	3. _____
220.3	4. _____	643.1 Am	4. _____
817.5	5. _____	643.3 Br	5. _____
641.1	6. _____	645.2 Tr	6. _____
811	7. _____	768.5 Br	7. _____
468.3	8. _____	398.2 Ta	8. _____
468.5	9. _____	398.2 Tn	9. _____
468.2	10. _____	398.2 Tr	10. _____

817.5 An	1. _____	817.5 Am	1. _____
974.5 Bl	2. _____	974.5 Br	2. _____
974.5 Ba	3. _____	817.5 Dr	3. _____
817.5 Ch	4. _____	817.5 Ch	4. _____
817.5 Dr	5. _____	974.5 Ba	5. _____
974.5 Br	6. _____	974.4 Bl	6. _____
817.5 Am	7. _____	817.5 An	7. _____
423.8 Ha	8. _____	808.9 Mo	8. _____
647.5 Mc	9. _____	826.7 Je	9. _____
419.9 Ke	10. _____	120.9 Ja	10. _____

DEWEY NUMBERS— CALL NUMBERS

A call number found on the spine of a book tells you where you can find that book on the library shelf. The number tells you what section of the library holds the book and the letters (the first two letters of the author's last name) tell you who wrote the book.

Example: All About the Planets by James P. Starburst has a call number of:

> 523
> St

Sometimes call numbers will have a decimal point.

Example: 523.3. This is just another way of dividing the sections again.

Call numbers are arranged in number order. Then the numbers following the point are put in order. And then the letters of the author's name are put in order.

Example: 523.1
523.5   Which comes first? *Answer:* 523.1

Example: 521.1
524.1   Which comes first? *Answer:* 512.1

Example: 523.1 Ab
523.1 Tr   Which comes first? *Answer:* 523.1 Ab

The key fact to remember is that you are using numbers and letters to organize the books on the library shelves.

DEWEY NUMBERS

Dewey call numbers are arranged in number order. Then the numbers following the point are put in order. And then the first two letters of the author's last name are put in order.

Example:

```
┌──────┐
│ 92.1 │
│ Ab   │
└──────┘
```

```
┌──────┐
│ 92.1 │
│ Wr   │
└──────┘
```
Which one comes first? *Answer:*   92.1
                                    Ab

Put these Dewey numbers in order.

817.5 Ch	1. _____		910.2 Ro	1. _____
817.5 Rd	2. _____		907.5 Ca	2. _____
974.4 Br	3. _____		901.4 Cr	3. _____
817.5 Am	4. _____		900.5 Tr	4. _____
974.5 Bl	5. _____		941.2 Br	5. _____
974.5 Ba	6. _____		953.5 Gr	6. _____
817.5 An	7. _____		936.6 Tr	7. _____

202.5 Br	1. _____		811 Ba	1. _____
801.4 Cr	2. _____		745.5 Ba	2. _____
971.5 Tr	3. _____		641.4 Br	3. _____
436.5 Ca	4. _____		941.5 To	4. _____
236.3 Cr	5. _____		920 Ro	5. _____
761.5 Ta	6. _____		921 Ro	6. _____
636.4 Ca	7. _____		438.6 La	7. _____

971.5 Tr	1. _____		974.5 Ba	1. _____
801.4 Cr	2. _____		974.5 Br	2. _____
761.5 Ta	3. _____		817.5 Dr	3. _____
636.4 Ca	4. _____		974.5 Bl	4. _____
436.5 Ca	5. _____		817.5 Ch	5. _____
236.3 Cr	6. _____		817.5 Am	6. _____
202.5 Br	7. _____		817.5 An	7. _____

NAME THAT DEWEY NUMBER AND SUBJECT

Read the following situations. Can you find the Dewey number and subject under which you could find a book to help you? *(Use the Dewey Decimal System Chart on page 20.)*

1. _____ Your dog insists upon stomping on the neighbors' flowers. How can you train your pet? Where do you look?

2. _____ You desperately want two white mice as pets. But your mom says mice are just too much trouble to care for and keep. Where can you find a book to help you?

3. _____ Your neighbor saw a shooting star. They have been star watching. Where can you find a book about stars?

4. _____ Your older sister plans to vote in the next election for president. Where can you find a book about the presidents?

5. _____ Your town will be part of the First Annual Ground Hog Day parade. Where do you find information about the history of Ground Hog Day?

6. _____ One of your classmates brought a chameleon to class. After placing it on the teacher's desk, it changed colors. Where can you find a book that explains these color changes?

7. _____ Your cousin plans to visit. He knows all about the latest music. Where can you find a book to help you "catch up?"

8. _____ You plan to bake something special for the holidays. But you need a really different recipe. Where do you look?

9. _____ You need a book about seashells for your science report. Where do you look?

10. _____ Your pet gerbil is a strange shade of color. Are you feeding it correctly? Where do you look?

NAME THAT DEWEY NUMBER AND SUBJECT

Read the situations below. How could you find the information that you need? Write the Dewey number and subject on the line. *(Use the Dewey Decimal System Chart on page 20.)*

1. _____ You plan to create a mask for the costume your are making. Your arts and craft work will help make your costume a hit. Where do you look?

2. _____ You want to learn beginning French. Where do you look?

3. _____ You just received a cute puppy. You want to take a picture of it, but do not know anything about photography. Where do you look?

4. _____ You plan to write a report for your science class. You plan to make a chart but do not know how to label the rocks in your report. Where do you look?

5. _____ Your cousin is visiting. And he knows all about the rules of football! How can you even the odds before you play? Where do you look?

6. _____ You plan to create a birthday card. You have an idea of what you will do but you need to look at some poems for your card. Where do you look?

7. _____ You need a book about the American Revolutionary War. Where do you look?

8. _____ You are concerned about what clothes to bring when your parents take you on vacation. You will be visiting Maine. Where do you look?

9. _____ New neighbors moved in. They practice the Hindu religion. Where do you look?

10. _____ You need to know if your library has an atlas (a book of maps). Where do you look?

OVERVIEW—
USING THE DEWEY DECIMAL SYSTEM

Use the Dewey Decimal System Chart on page 20 to answer the following questions. Give the subject and number for each question.

1. _____ You plan to draw the ships and treasures of the early explorers.

2. _____ You plan to set up a rock display for extra credit in science.

3. _____ You have just met the new student in class. He speaks French. Where do you look for a book that will tell you how to say "hello?"

4. _____ Your pet canary has not sung a song in a week. Are you feeding him correctly?

5. _____ Your family is moving. You will be going to Maine. But you do not know a single fact about the state. Where do you look?

Read the following book titles. In what Dewey division will you find them?

1. _____ *Insects and Their Homes*

2. _____ *How a Law is Made*

3. _____ *Plays for Young People*

4. _____ *Fairy Tales of Foreign Lands*

5. _____ *Soccer*

6. _____ *The Care of Hamsters and Mice*

7. _____ *Travelling through India*

8. _____ *The Life of Walt Disney*

9. _____ *Cooking for Kids*

How would these call numbers be arranged on the library shelf?

1. 791.1 Ba   _____

2. 790.1 Br   _____

3. 345.1 Ta   _____

4. 401.5 Tr   _____

5. 201.5 Br   _____

PARTS OF A BOOK

Everything you see is made of parts. A bicycle, a car, a television, and a stereo all are made of smaller units. When they are put together in a logical, orderly way, a useful product is made. If you were to look at any one of the examples listed, and break it down into its components, you would better understand how and why the product works. A book is no exception.

A book is made of parts too. Each helps the book work. Look at the cover of a book. What do you see? The title, the author, and perhaps the illustrator's name. Now open the book and turn the page. The title page and copyright page are the first pages you will see. They present the full title of the book, the author, and the publisher. Now turn the page. The table of contents presents you with a brief introduction of what you can expect to find in the book. Turn the next page. The book might have a preface. Not all books will have a preface. This book part is usually very short. It explains what important facts or thoughts that the author has and wants you to know about. For example, if the author wrote a book about ants, he might want to explain in the preface that he wrote the book because he was always fascinated by insects as a child. He may have developed several friendships with people who study insects. And they may have helped in the writing of the book. The author may mention this in the preface. Now turn the page.

The main part of the book is called the body of the book. This is "the book." It has all the information you will need. It is the largest part of the book. Turn all those pages. Now look at the front part of the book. This is sometimes overlooked by students. It does contain important information for you. The book may have an illustration page. This is a list of illustrations and the page numbers where you can find them in the book. At the back of the book may be an appendix. This is any body of information that the author would like you to refer to in the book. For example, if that book about ants has several charts showing where ants can be found throughout the world, the author may include this information in an appendix.

And a glossary may follow these pages. A glossary is like a mini-dictionary. It lists in alphabetical order all the important terms presented in the book. And each term is explained. This part of the book can be very helpful to you. It will allow you to check any word or term you are uncertain of without reading an entire chapter to find it.

The index is the last part of the back matter or back part of the book. It is an alphabetical listing of all important or key subjects discussed in the book. In this list you will also find names or titles discussed in the book.

You see that all the parts of a book work together for you. You can get information that will help you from each part. Now let's look at specific parts, and learn how to use them.

THE COPYRIGHT PAGE

The copyright page is the back side of the title page. What does it have? Let's look at the title page. The title page will give you the title, author, illustrator, publisher, and place of publication. If your book has no author but has an editor it will be on this page. An editor may be responsible for putting the work of several authors together in one book. If that is the case, his name goes on the title page.

Now turn this page. You are looking at the copyright page. This page tells you when the book was copyrighted. What does this mean? Let's compare it to something you know much about—yourself. When you were born or officially became part of the world, you were given a date. This date is called your birthdate. Think of a copyright date as the official birthdate of a book. It is the date that the book officially becomes part of the world.

Why is it so important to know what the copyright date of a book is? It tells you something about the information in that book. Let's say that your birthdate tells us that you are eleven years old. We know that you are in fifth grade and we know exactly how long you have been around. The copyright date of a book works the same way. If you are writing a report about ants and you have two books, look at the copyright dates. Let's say one is published in 1988 and the other in 1938. Which book would you expect to have more information? The book that is one year old or the book that is fifty years old. The 1988 book, of course, would have the latest information. Is there ever a time when this information would be very important?

Yes. Let's say that you are writing a report about the latest developments in the space field. You choose several books from your library. One book was published in 1965, one book in 1975, and one book in 1988. Which one will you choose? If you are writing about the latest developments, you would choose the 1988 book. Why? It has the latest information about space. If you are more interested in the developments in the space field and the history of them, what would you choose? The 1965 book would be more helpful to you. It would have more about the history of the development in space research. Do you see why the copyright page can be helpful to you?

Let's pretend that you have finished writing your report. Your teacher asks you what is the title of the book and who wrote it? She also would like to know where it was published and by whom? Where do you get all this information? Turn that copyright page back and look at the title page. It will give you all the information that you need. And if your teacher asks you to write this information at the end of your report (we call this a bibliography) you will know where to get it.

Now you see why the title and copyright pages are important parts of a book Let's look more closely at these book parts and learn how to use them.

USING THE TITLE AND COPYRIGHT PAGE

You will need these sample pages for the questions on page 34.

The Mystery of the Purple Shoes

by
Harriet B. Sole

Illustrated by
Linda Heel Toe

Mystery Press
Strangetown, New Jersey

Copyright © 1993 by Mystery Press

NAME _____

USING THE COPYRIGHT AND TITLE PAGE

Read the copyright and title pages. You will be able to answer the questions below. *(Use the sample pages on page 33.)*

1. When was the book published?   _____

2. Who wrote the book?   _____

3. Is there an illustrator for this book? If so, who?   _____

4. What is the title of this book?   _____

5. Who published this book?   _____

6. Where was this book published?   _____

Using Copyright Dates for Your Reports

1. You found two books for your report about the planet Venus. The copyright date is 1941 for *Venus: The Strange Planet* and 1989 for *Venus: Bright Planet*. Which one would be a better choice for your report about the latest information?   _____

2. Look at the copyright dates for these books. Which one would be the best choice for a report about the latest information about nutrition? _____

    Vitamins, 1970
    Eating for Good Health, 1989
    Your Body and Nutrition, 1976
    Vitamins and Minerals, 1981

3. Look at the copyright dates for these books. Which two books would be your best choice for a report about the latest space developments?

                                                          _____

    Space Today, 1979
    Space Frontiers, 1989   _____
    Working in Space, 1987
    Our Plans for Space Travel, 1980

4. You are writing a report about the history of the space program. What book would be your best choice?

    Space Travel: A History, 1959   _____
    Space History, 1958
    Space Programs, 1959

THE TABLE OF CONTENTS

The table of contents page follows the title and copyright page. It can give you important information quickly and easily. The table of contents gives you a general idea of what is in the book. We call these chapter headings. You might like to think of them as titles of each chapter that you will find in the book.

How can a table of contents help you? Let's say that you are writing a report about ants. You stand before the science shelves in your library and see ten books about ants. Do you read them all? Of course not, that is unless you have the time or the desire to do so. So how do you find which books will help you without reading them all? You use the table of contents in each book. Turn to the table of contents page. Read the chapter headings. Are they going to be helpful? How do you decide?

Let's say that your report about ants will be about how they build their nests. Let's look at a sample table of contents. Then you decide what chapters will be most helpful.

CHAPTER ONE   What is an ant?
CHAPTER TWO   Why ants build nests
CHAPTER THREE   Where ants build their nests
CHAPTER FOUR   How ants build their nests
CHAPTER FIVE   What ants eat
CHAPTER SIX   Types of ants
CHAPTER SEVEN   Where ants are found throughout the world

Look at this table of contents. What chapters will be helpful to you? Chapter two, chapter three, and chapter four, will help you.

You need to know if ants are found in South America. Table of contents or index? Think about this question. Is it a general fact that you are looking for or a more specific one? It is a specific detail. Where do you look? The index. You may have to read the entire page or pages of the index. Why? Because you may not know under what subject this information would be listed? What might you try? "Ants, location throughout the world" would be an excellent listing. But what if it is not written that way? Do you give up? No. Your information may be listed under "ants, places found in" or "ants where can be found." So you see you must read the index not just look at parts of it for the information you need.

Let's look at one more. Let's say you need information about the worker ant. Where do you look? The table of contents or the index? The worker ant is a type of ant. Let's first check the table of contents. Is there a chapter about types of ants? If so, turn to the chapter. You may need to read the entire chapter to see if there is enough information for your report. If there is, fine. But what if the chapter is a short one and it does not discuss this particular type of ant? Where do you look? That's right. The index. What do you look under? Types of ants? Worker ants? Both are good. You might try them both. If there is information in the book, it will tell on what page you may look.

Remember: the table of contents presents general information. The index is more specific. Choose the one that fits your needs. Do you need specific information? Or do you need general information? Ask yourself these questions before you turn those pages.

THE TABLE OF CONTENTS

Let's look at one more table of contents.

CHAPTER ONE	The ant's body parts
CHAPTER TWO	Types of ants
CHAPTER THREE	Where ants are found in the world
CHAPTER FOUR	What ants eat
CHAPTER FIVE	Enemies of the ants
CHAPTER SIX	The queen ant
CHAPTER SEVEN	Ants and their jobs in the nest

Look at this table of contents carefully. Is there anything listed that would help in your report? No, there is not. So you have learned by reading a table of contents that a book may be titled *Ants* but not have the information you need.

What do you do first? Decide exactly what you are looking for in the writing of your report. Know your subject. Then read the table of contents page for your subject. It is that easy.

Remember you do not have to read the entire book in order to find the information that you want. But you do need to know how the parts of a book work and how to use them.

Let's look closely at the table of contents page and learn how to use it.

THE INDEX

Imagine what it would be like if none of our information was in order. What would it be like if you opened a telephone book and saw all the names listed in no particular order at all? Confusing. You would spend hours trying to find the phone number you needed. That is, if you found it at all. But put these names in an order such as alphabetical order, and it is simple to find the numbers you need.

If you try to use a library without knowing how the information is placed in order, you may have the same problem. All the information in a library is put in order. Let's find out how, so we can use it well. The index is very important in a library because it helps put information in order. You can reduce the amount of time you spend in the library looking for information.

An index is a list of topics or subjects. It is in alphabetical order. The list gives specific information. It gives details. It is different from a table of contents. A table of contents gives general information.

So where do you find the index? In a book it is in the back after the main part of the book. The encyclopedia has a book after the last volume. It is called the index. Mazazines often have the index at the back, also. And the newspaper will have the index on the back of the first page.

Let's try to use the index. If you needed to find information about how large the eyes of a horse are, where would you go? Would you use the table of contents or the index? Why? Think about it. Do you need a specific detail or a general fact? You could read the table of contents in a book to find a chapter heading that may help you. Or you could read the index at the back of the book. What would you look under? If the subject horses-eyes were listed, you would find the page number after it. It would be easier if you used the index.

Let's say you plan to write a report about how to take care of horses. Your report will be more than one page. Will you go to an index or a table of contents? Think about what you need. Do you need specific information? Do you need general information? How much information do you need?

You would choose the table of contents. Why? You need general information. You need quite a bit of information. The table of contents will give you a good idea what is in the book. The index will give you a specific list of details or subjects in the book.

But what if you decide to include how to exercise a horse? You could read a complete chapter about horse care. It might be in the chapter. Or you could read the index. Check the index. Let's say the subject horses-exercise is listed. The page number where you can find this information will follow the words. Turn to the page. You have your information.

Let's look at one more. Your teacher assigns a report about ants. How can you spend your library time wisely? Your teacher would like you to use information from four different source. You will use the book, encyclopedia, magazine, and the newspaper. How can you get this information quickly?

You can use the indexes. Are these indexes all the same? Let's look at each type of index.

THE BOOK INDEX

You stand before the science section of your library. And you see the books about ants. Your report will be about how ants build their nest. Do you read all ten books? You can read the table of contents in each book. There may be a chapter on nest building. But maybe the information about nest building is part of a larger chapter. Or maybe there is only one small paragraph about nest building in the entire book. How do you find out? Use the book index.

Turn to the back of the book. Remember the index is in alphabetical order. Find ants, nest building. And look at the page number after the subject ants, nest building. It will look like this:

ants, nest building, p. 30–34

How many pages of information are in this book for your report? Pages 30, 31, 32, 33, 34. Five pages for your report.

Repeat this process for any other book you choose on those library shelves. You will find the information you need and you will find it quickly.

Let's look at some sample book indexes. You will learn how to use them.

THE INDEX PAGE

An index is much longer than a table of contents because it covers the subjects listed in the book. But lets say that we are looking at this index to answer our question about ants and their building habits. Would this book help?

If we look at page 39-40, we will find information about their ways of building nests. So this book would be of help to you.

Lets look at another example.

ants, body parts	p. 3, 37, 40
ants, brown	p. 17, 39
ants, nests	p. 39–42
ants, enemies	p. 31, 32, 33
ants, food	p. 5, 6, 7
ants, red	p. 3
ants, spiders	p. 67–71
ants, termites	p. 87
ants, their helpfulness to people	p. 89–94
ants, throughout (places found) the world	p. 117–123

THE BOOK INDEX

ANTS

ants, body parts	p. 3, 37, 40
ants, brown	p. 17, 39
ants, enemies	p. 31, 32, 33
ants, food	p. 5, 6, 7
ants, homes	p. 39–42
ants, red	p. 3
ants, spiders	p. 67–71
ants, termites	p. 87
ants, their helpfulness to people	p. 89–94
ants, throughout (places found) the world	p. 117–123

On what page would you expect to find the information to answer the following questions?

1. _____ You need information about ants and the desert. Can ants be found in deserts or dry climates?

2. _____ You are drawing a cover for your report about ants. You plan to draw at least two types of ants. What two listings will help you?

3. _____ Your cousin is studying ant hills. How do ants build ant hills? Where do you look?

4. _____ You plan to make a model of an ant for the science fair. But you are not certain how many body parts an ant has. What listing will give you exact information about what an ant looks like?

5. _____ Do ants ever eat green leaves? Where do you look?

6. _____ Are spiders friends or enemies of ants?

7. _____ Your parents saw flying ants outside the house. Are they flying ants or termites?

8. _____ Your little brother is just about to step on an ant hill. "Stop!" You say. "Don't you know that ants help people?" What listing will give you more facts?

9. _____ Do birds like ants? Where do you look?

10. _____ What is the difference between an ant and a termite?

USING A BOOK INDEX

Read the book index below.

ANTS	
ants, the body	p. 5
ants, the nest	p. 7
ants, and people	p. 9
ants, food	p. 13
ants, location of the nest	p. 15
ants, types	p. 17
ants, worker	p. 19
ants, queen	p. 23
ants, their enemies	p. 27
ants, and the weather	p. 31

Read the following questions. You can find where to get the answers by reading the book index. Some questions will have more than one page number for an answer.

1. _____ On what pages can you find information about the places where ants might make their nests?

2. _____ Is a drone a type of ant?

3. _____ Are spiders friendly towards ants?

4. _____ Are green plants a good food source for ants?

5. _____ Does an ant have three or five major body parts?

6. _____ Is a damp area a favorable place for ants to build their nests?

7. _____ Who is the leader of an ant colony?

8. _____ How long do worker ants live?

9. _____ Is there information in this book about the difference between red and brown ants?

10. _____ Can insects be friends of ants?

11. _____ Are nests ever built in dry places?

12. _____ Is there such an ant as the nurse ant?

13. _____ Is there a special way in which the ant colony is made?

USING A BOOK INDEX

Read the book index below. Notice how much information it has.

Afghan hounds 20, 24	breeds of dogs, special 27
American Kennel Club 19	eyesight 22
avalanche rescue dogs 20, 21	face language 28
baby dogs, 22, 26	guide dogs 27
basset hound 27, 31	hearing, sense of 22
beauty parlors for dogs 31	rescue dogs 25
breeds of dogs and their ancestors 23	tail language 34
breeds of dogs, illustrated 24, 25	training dogs 58
breeds of dogs, number of 19	working with man 72

You are looking for information about dogs. Check the book index. Answer the following questions.

1. _____ What pages will give you information about rescue dogs?

2. _____ On what page can you find information about the number of breeds of dogs?

3. _____ Can you find information about dog grooming?

4. _____ Can you find information about the history of dogs?

5. _____ Is there any information about a dog's sense of taste?

6. _____ What four listings give information about how dogs can be useful to man?

7. _____ What listing will give you information about what dogs look like?

8. _____ What two listings will give you information about a dog's senses?

9. _____ Can you find information about the American Kennel Club?

10. _____ Are there special breeds of dogs? Name the listing.

11. _____ Do dogs talk with their tails?

12. _____ Where can you find information about where to take your dog to make him/her beautiful?

13. _____ Where can you find pictures of dogs?

COMPARING
TABLE OF CONTENTS
AND INDEX

It is important that you understand the difference between the table of contents and the index parts of a book. Both can be very helpful to you. But they are very different. You will use the table of contents when you are interested in a general piece of information. You will use the index when you want a specific piece of information. What does this mean?

Let's say that you need to find how many body parts an ant has. If you are looking at the table of contents page and see "ants, the body," you are in luck. But what if you can not find a chapter heading such as this one. Where do you look? Check the index. You may look under ants, body parts. If you find this listing, you are in luck. If not, you may want to look under another subject. You may look under ants, structure of the body, or maybe under body parts. You will have to think about this a bit because there is no clear-cut method of indexing subjects.

Odds are that the subjects that come to your mind first are a good place to start. What if you have checked both the table of contents and the index and do not find a place where the information is listed? Find another book. Start looking again. Begin with the table of contents if you need general information and turn to the index if you need more specific information.

Let's look at some sample questions. See if you can decide where you should turn to; the table of contents or the index.

COMPARING CONTENTS
AND INDEX PAGES

(Use with page 47 & 48.)

CONTENTS

CHAPTER 1
What is a Bee?

CHAPTER 2
How Bees Live

CHAPTER 3
Workers

CHAPTER 4
Queens and Drones

CHAPTER 5
More Bees

INDEX

antennae 8
abdomen 8, 25
beeswax 12, 34
body 8
bumblebee 11
colony 10, 38
comb 19
drone 12, 28, 34, 36, 38
eggs 29, 33, 34, 36
feelers 8
glands 8, 34
hive 10, 38
larva 34, 36
nectar 22, 24
pollen 8, 20, 21
pupa 36
queen 12, 38, 30, 33, 35, 37
royal jelly 35
scouts 14
sting 8, 25
stomach 23
swarm 14–16

NAME _____

COMPARING THE INDEX
AND TABLE OF CONTENTS

Read the following questions. You may find the answers by reading the sample index page and reading the table of contents page found on page 46. Remember each part of the book will help you.

1. _____ What will give you more detailed information—the table of contents or the index?

2. _____ If you have a specific topic to search for, which will help you get the information more quickly and easily?

3. _____ If you want a general idea of what information can be found what will help you?

4. _____ You need to find information about a specific detail for your report. Where do you go?

5. _____ You need to skim the book for a specific detail for your report. Where do you go?

6. _____ Why is the index written in alphabetical order?

7. _____ You need to know what a bee's tongue is like? Where do you go?

8. _____ You need to know on what pages you can find specific facts about the worker. Where do you go?

9. _____ How do bees swarm? On what pages would you find this information?

10. _____ What is the queen bee like? On what pages would you find this information?

COMPARING THE INDEX AND
THE TABLE OF CONTENTS

Compare the index and the table of contents found on page 46. Answer the following questions.

1. _____ You need information about how bees make wax. Where do you look?

2. _____ You need information about why bees swarm. Where do you look?

3. _____ Is there any information about bumblebees?

4. _____ Is there any information about how bees form colonies?

5. _____ Where can you find information about the queen bee in the table of contents? In the index?

6. _____ Is there such bees as scout bees? Where do you look?

7. _____ Can you find any information about bees and pollen? Where do you look?

8. _____ Can you find any information about the sting of a bee? Where do you look?

9. _____ Can you find any information about how a bee builds a hive? Where do you look?

10. _____ You need information about the drone. Where do you look in the table of contents? In the index?

THE ILLUSTRATION PAGE

What is the illustration page? Why is it an important part of a book? The illustration page gives you some information quickly and easily that you might need for your report. Let's say that your report about ants is coming along just fine. But as you read it, you decide that you need some pictures. You decide that a picture of ants building their nests would be good. And you also decide that a picture of the red and brown ant would add to your report. How do you get this information quickly? Check the illustration page.

The illustration page is a list of all the illustrations or pictures that you will find in the book. It will tell the page you can find each illustration on. Where can you find the illustration page? It usually is in the back of the book. How can it be useful to you? Let's go back to our example of the red and brown ants. Read the illustration page. Under what heading will you find the information that you need? Brown ants, red ants, ant nests, ant homes, types of ant homes; any of these are possible headings you may check. Let's look at a sample illustration page.

ants, body parts	page 7
ants, brown	page 8
ants, building nests	page 10
ants, drone	page 9
ants, red	page 5
ants, queen	page 6
ants, worker	page 11

What pages will help you? Pages 8, 9, and 10 will give you the pictures that you need for your report. And you did not have to read the entire book to find them. Use the illustration page the next time you need a picture for your report.

Let's look at another example.

ants, antennae	page 8
ants, body parts	page 3
ants, drones	page 7
ants, queen	page 9
ants, worker	page 12

Is there any information about red or brown ants? No. Will this book give you the pictures you need for your report? No. Go to another book. Check the illustration page. It will tell you the information you need to know. Now let's look closely at the illustration page. Learn how to use it.

NAME _____

USING THE ILLUSTRATION PAGE

Read the illustration page below.

ILLUSTRATION LIST

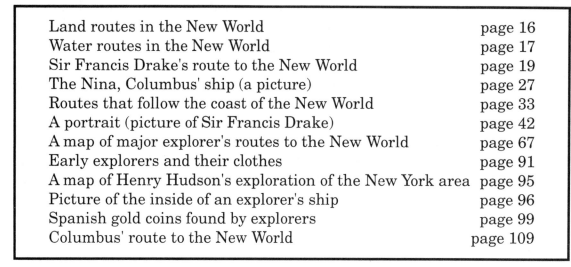

Land routes in the New World	page 16
Water routes in the New World	page 17
Sir Francis Drake's route to the New World	page 19
The Nina, Columbus' ship (a picture)	page 27
Routes that follow the coast of the New World	page 33
A portrait (picture of Sir Francis Drake)	page 42
A map of major explorer's routes to the New World	page 67
Early explorers and their clothes	page 91
A map of Henry Hudson's exploration of the New York area	page 95
Picture of the inside of an explorer's ship	page 96
Spanish gold coins found by explorers	page 99
Columbus' route to the New World	page 109

1. _____ You need a cover for your report. You plan to draw a Spanish helmut. Where might you look?

2. _____ You need a map of the land explored by Hudson. Where do you look?

3. _____ What two pictures will help you write a report about Columbus?

   _____

4. _____ How many pictures or illustrations are in this book about Sir Francis Drake?

5. _____ You will draw one of Columbus' ships as a cover for your report. Where do you look?

6. _____ Did Pizarro sail along the coast of Florida?

7. _____ What did explorers bring with them to the New World?

8. _____ You will report about the explorer, John Cabot. What route did he take to the New World?

9. _____ What did the treasure look like that the explorers found in the New World?

10. _____ Your report is about Sir Francis Drake. Is there a picture of him?

THE GLOSSARY

What is a glossary? Where do you find it in a book? It is like a mini-dictionary for the new or difficult words in the book. You will find it at the back of the book. It is in alphabetical order. When do you use the glossary? You can use it in several ways.

Let's say that you do not understand completely a word you wrote in your report. You are writing about the nest building habits of the brown ant. The book used the word antennae. You wrote it down but forgot to explain what it is. How can you get that information quickly? Check the glossary. Find the word antennae. It will define it for you. You see the glossary works like a small dictionary for select words in the body of the book.

Let's look at part of a sample glossary.

Body parts—The ant has three major body parts.
Drone—the worker ant in the nest.
Queen—the leader of the ant colony.

1. What does a drone do in the ant colony?
    He is the worker in the colony.

2. How many major body parts do ants have?
    The ant has three major body parts.

3. Who is the leader in the ant colony?
    The queen ant is the leader.

Always remember: you need not search the book for a word. Use the glossary.

NAME _____

THE GLOSSARY

A glossary is a mini-dictionary found at the back of the book. It explains key words found in the body of the book. You can use it to find information quickly. Use the glossary at the back of this book to answer the following questions.

1. What is the difference between a **play** and a **poem**? _____
    _____

2. What is the difference between **science fiction** and **fantasy**? _____
    _____

3. How is a **glossary** different from an **index**? _____
    _____

4. Which gives more detailed information an **index** or a **table of contents**?
    Define each term. _____
    _____

5. What is the difference between an **encyclopedia see also cross refer-**
    ence and **heading**? _____
    _____

6. What information does a **bibliography** give? _____
    _____

7. What is the difference between **fiction** and **nonfiction**? _____
    _____

8. What is the purpose of **guide letters**? _____
    _____

9. What is a **media card**? _____
    _____

MAGAZINES

There are over eighty children's magazines. Some are specialized and cover science, history, world studies, etc.; others contain more general information. Reading a magazine may be a refreshing change from reading an entire book—with a magazine you can start and finish a story or article in one sitting. Magazines are also up-to-date and express a variety of opinions.

Magazines are sometimes referred to as *periodicals* because they are published at regular intervals: weekly, bi-weekly, monthly, bi-monthly, or quarterly.

Choose a magazine and fill in the following information:

Name of magazine: _____ Date: _____

Does the magazine have a table of contents? _____

Are the contents listed by departments? _____

If so, what are the names of the departments listed? _____

_____

_____

What is the cost of a single copy? _____
(Note: Not all magazines are sold individually.)

What is the cost for a yearly subscription? _____

What would you pay for this magazine if you lived in Canada? _____

What is the copyright date of the magazine? _____

How often is the magazine published? _____

What is the address of the magazine publisher? _____

_____

Who is the main editor of this magazine? _____
(An editor is the person in charge of writing and publishing the magazine.)

Volume: All copies of a magazine published during one year have the same volume number.

Number: Each copy of a magazine is numbered beginning with 1 for the first copy of the year, 2 for the second, etc.

What is the volume of your magazine? _____ The number? _____

The MAGAZINE Table of Contents Page

Questions and Answers about the Chinook Indians page 6
> by Ellen Harsog

Struggle for a Homeland—A History .... page 10
> by Kathleen Burk

Cherokee Basket Game and Activity .... page 15

Sequoia and the Talking Leaves .... page 16
> by Peter Doop

The Trail of Tears—The Cherokee Removal .... page 20
> by Elizabeth Tenny

The Great Chiefs .... page 28
> by Elizabeth West

Borrowed Names—Indian Word Game .... page 31
> by Peg Schabel

Read the questions below. Write the name of the magazine article and the page number where you would find this information.

1. _____ What article will give you some of the history of the Cherokee Indians?

2. _____ Can you find any information about Indian myths? If so, on what page?

3. _____ On what pages can you find information about Indian names?

4. _____ What is the title of the article on page 16?

5. _____ Is there any information about Indian crafts in this issue? If so, on what page?

6. _____ Is there any information about Indian games in this issue? If so, on what page?

7. _____ "The Great Chiefs," begins on what page?

8. _____ What article would give you information about the Chinook tribe?

9. _____ Which article is written by Elizabeth West?

10. _____ "The Trail of Tears" tells what about the Cherokee Indians?

THE CHILDREN'S MAGAZINE GUIDE

In addition to all of the books in the library, magazines may also be useful tools for locating information, especially *recent* information on topics you are researching.

In order to use magazine effectively, getting to know the *Children's Magazine Guide* (Published by R.R. Bowker) will be helpful.

- The guide is arranged by subject alphabetically. The headings are in all capital letters in bold-faced type. (*Example:* **WOLVERINES**)

- If you want to look up a review on a book or a movie, look under **BOOK REVIEWS** or **MOVIE REVIEWS**. the titles will be listed alphabetically under these headings.

- Other general topic headings include **HUMOROUS POETRY, LIMERICKS, NONSENSE VERSES, CHILDREN'S STORIES & POETRY** (stories and poetry *written by* children), and **PLAYS**.

- If you can't find your topic listed in the guide, try to think of another heading that is similar (Example: for information on fossils, try **ARCHEOLOGY, DINOSAURS, EXCAVATIONS (Archeology), FOSSILS, PREHISTORIC ANIMALS**.

subject ———— Camps: see also Camping ———— *cross reference*
title of article ———— Real Kids Looking on the Bright Side.
note —————————— (Summer camp for the visually handicapped)
         E.B. Senisi. U* S * Kids Jun '93 p32–33—*page numbers*
author   *magazine*   *date*

Here are some tips for reading the entries:

- The cross-reference will tell you where to find more information on this topic in the *Children's Magazine Guide*.

- The note will give you additional information about the article.

- Sometimes the magazines are abbreviated—the full name can be found on the inside front cover of the *Children's Magazine Guide*.

- After the page number you may see a "+." This means that the article is continued later in the magazine.

These are the abbreviations for the months of the year in the *Children's Magazine Guide*: Jan, Feb, Mar, Apr, May, Jun, Jul, Aug, Sep, Oct, Nov, Dec.

NAME _____

CHILDREN'S MAGAZINE GUIDE

Choose an entry on any subject from a magazine which we get in the library. Search a column of entries for the name of a magazine you can find useful.

Subject _____

Copy the complete entry.

_____
Title

_____   _____
Author   Magazine

_____   _____
Date   Pages

Locate the magazine in the library. Place your paper in the magazine and put them on top of the card catalog.

Remember: It is possible that the magazine is signed out. So, if you cannot find it after a reasonable search, just turn in your paper.

USING A MAGAZINE GUIDE

DINOSAURS
Bones, C.W. Bone. Fossil Magazine. Jan '87 p. 27–29
Bones, Fossils and the Donosaurs. Dinosaur Magazine. July '86 p. 65
How the Dinosaurs Lived. History Magazine. Sept. '89 p. 34
How the Dinosaur Found Food. History Magazine. Sept. '88 p. 21.
Plants and the Dinosaurs. Fossil Magazine. Sept. '89 p. 17.
Pictures of Prehistoric Dinosaurs. Art Magazine. Nov. '86 p. 17
Poems About Dinosaurs. Poetry Magazine. June '87 p. 13
Songs and Plays About Dinosaurs for Children. Children's Magazine.
    April '89 p. 33
The Truth About Dinosaurs. Dinosaur Magazine. May '87 p. 3
The Truth About Why Dinosaurs Disappeared. Dinosaur and Reptile
    Magazine. June '87 p. 27

1. _____ What magazine will give you poems about the dinosaurs?

2. _____ You need several pictures for your report about dinosaurs. What magazine would give you the most help?

3. _____ Your younger brother will be in a play about dinosaurs. He plans to sing a song about dinosaurs. What magazine will help him?

4. _____ Why did dinosaurs disappear? What magazine will help?

5. _____ What plants existed during dinosaur times? What magazine will help?

6. _____ Your younger sister plans to build a model of a dinosaur for the science fair. What magazine will give her ideas of what the dinosaur looked like?

7. _____
   _____ You plan to make a food chain chart for the dinosaur. Where can you find out what dinosaurs ate? Name *two* magazines.

8. _____
   _____ What *two* articles were printed in History Magazine?

MAGAZINES
WRITING TO BE PUBLISHED

Many children's magazines accept contributions from young authors and artists. Such contributions include: stories, nonfiction, poetry, riddles, jokes, profiles, interviews, letters to the editor, contents, and artwork. A few magazines will offer payment, others offer prizes, and most will offer free copies of the magazine issue with your work in it.

Here are some steps to follow when submitting a piece of your work to a magazine.

1. Have students decide which is their best manuscript and/or piece of art.

2. Select a magazine best-suited to the manuscript. Select two additional markets. On a sheet of paper, write the three markets in order. Clip to manuscript. Do the same for artwork.

3. Prepare manuscript to submit to a publisher. Be sure to follow the publisher's guidelines. Note the word-length requirements.

   If you plan to submit your material for publication continue with these activities.

4. Check to see if the publisher requires a parent or teacher signature. Address an envelope to the publisher and enclose a stamped, self-addressed envelope. Add sufficient postage and mail manuscript. Add the submission date to the market sheet in your "Writer's Guidebook."

5. Be patient! It may take as long as three months for a response.

6. Start another writing project.

7. If your manuscript is returned with a rejection slip, do not be discouraged. Send it off immediatley to the next magazine on your list. Record the date it was returned and the date resubmitted to the next publisher.

MARKET LIST

This market list is given only as a guide. There are many other magazines, newsletters, and quarterly publications that accept materials from young contributors. For an expanded and comprehensive listing, see the Young Writer's/Illustrator's market section of *Children's Writer's & Illustrator's Market* (Writer's Digest Books, 1992) Students wishing to contribute materials to magazines should write for the contributor's guidelines for young people and read current issues of the magazine. Magazines frequently change editors, addresses and even cease publication.

BOY'S LIFE
Box 152079
Irving, TX 75015-2079
　　Fiction, nonfiction, poetry

CHILDREN'S ALBUM
Box 6086
Concord, CA 94524
　　Fiction, artwork

CHILDREN'S DIGEST
Box 567
Indianapolis, IN 46206
　　Fiction, poems, riddles, letters

CHILDREN'S PLAYMATE
Box 567
Indianapolis, IN 46206
　　Poems, jokes, riddles, letters

CLUBHOUSE
Box 15
Berrien Springs, MI 49103
　　Fiction, nonfiction, poetry, artwork

CREATIVE KIDS
Box 6448
Mobile, AL 36660
　　Fiction, nonfiction, poetry, plays, artwork

HIGHLIGHTS FOR CHILDREN
803 Church Street
Honesdale, PA 18431
　　Science letters, favorite books, recipes, special features, artwork

MERLYN'S PEN
National Magazine of Student Writing
Box 1058
East Grenwich, RI 02818
　　Fiction, nonfiction, plays, letters to the editor, book reviews, artwork

MY FRIEND
50 St. Paul Avenue
Boston, MA 02130
　　"Junior Reporter" feature gives opportunity for students to suggest topics and do the research for an article.

PURPLE COW
350 Piedmont Road NE, Suite 415
Atlanta, GA 30305
　　Nonfiction, artwork

SCHOLASTIC SCOPE
730 Broadway
New York, NY 10003
　　Fiction, nonfiction, poetry

STONE SOUP
Box 83
Stanta Cruz, CA 95063
　　Fiction, poetry, artwork

STRAIGHT MAGAZINE
Standard Publishing
8121 Hamilton Avenue
Cincinnati, OH 45231
　　Fiction, poetry, artwork

SUNSHINE MAGAZINE
Box 40
Sunshine Park
Litchfield, IL 62056

WOMBAT: A JOURNAL OF YOUNG PEOPLE'S WRITING AND ART
365 Ashton Drive
Athens, GA 30606
　　Fiction, nonfiction, cartoons, puzzles, jokes, games, artwork

YOUNG VOICES MAGAZINE
P.O. Box 2321
Olympic, WA 98507
　　Fiction, nonfiction, book reviews, poetry, artwork

CANADIAN MAGAZINES

CHICKADEE & OWL MAGAZINES
56 The Esplanade #304
Toronto, Ontario,
Canada M5E 1A7

RANGER RICK
Canadian Wildlife Federation
1673 Carling Ave.
Ottawa, Ontario
Canada K2A 3Z1

SOMEWHERE TODAY
Youth Editions
P.O. Box 1310, Station B
Hull, Quebec
Canada J8X 3Y1

TREE HOUSE
The Young Naturalist Foundation
56 The Esplanade #304
Toronto, Ontario,
Canada M5E 1A7

THE NEWSPAPER INDEX

Now that you have information about ants' nests from books and encyclopedias, let's see if you can find information from a newspaper. Is there anything in your library about ants?

Maybe your library has more than one newspaper. Do you read each one cover to cover? Let's look at one newspaper. How do you check the newspaper for this information? You check the index.

Every newspaper has an index. Look at the inside of the front page. There is a list of articles and columns. These are in alphabetical order.

What is an article? It is a newspaper story. What is a column? It is a short article written regularly. Often it is written by the same person. You will find the articles and columns in sections of the newspaper. The newspaper is divided into parts or sections. Each section is given a letter. The subjects are listed alphabetically by section. The page number will follow the section letter. Let's say you choose a Sunday newspaper. There is a science section in the newspaper. Its letter is S, look under S in the index. It should look like this—S Science Today.

Animals in Our Environment	S 87
Let's Look at the Stars	S 91
Ants: Common Insects Build Homes	S 94

You are in luck. Turn to page 94 in the S section. Now let's look closely at the newspaper index and learn how to use it.

USING A NEWSPAPER INDEX

Read the newspaper index below.

FEATURES

Athlete of the Week	H 9
Arts and Crafts	C 13
Chess	C 15
Coins	C 16
Commuter News	A 25
Crossword Puzzle	A 29
Dining Out	E 4
Editorials	F 9
Home Sales	C 2
Movie Mini-Reviews	F 2
Movie Time Table	F 2
Music	F 6
News Quiz	G 5
Personal Computers	D 15
Record Reviews	F 6
Sports on T.V.	H 2
Your Health	B 15

(Use with page 62.)

USING A NEWSPAPER INDEX

Read the newspaper index on page 61. Look at the questions. What section of the paper and what page would you turn to for the information?

1. _____ Name the *two* feature articles in the "A" section.

   _____

2. _____ Is there a feature article on personal computers? On what page?

3. _____ "Chess" and "Coins" are features in what section?

4. _____ You wish to test your knowledge of news. What section will help you?

5. _____ What's on television tonight? Any sport specials?

6. _____ What section will tell you about peoples' letters to the editor?

7. _____ You want to keep a check on your favorite athlete. Is he the athlete of the week? Where do you find that information?

8. _____ What time does tonight's movie begin?

9. _____ You want to try a new place to eat. Where can you get some suggestions?

10. _____ What is the latest news about records?

11. _____ What feature will you find in section "A25?"

12. _____ You hear that the latest movie is really terrific. What does the critic say? Where do you look?

13. _____ You want your skin to look perfect for the dance. Where might you get some tips on your skin care?

14. _____ Your friend loves records. You want to buy the latest one. Where do you look?

15. _____ Your friend wrote a letter to the editor. Did they print it? Where do you look?

ENCYCLOPEDIAS

Encyclopedias are classified in the Dewey Decimal System as "generalities" and are found in the 030 section, unless they are kept in a special area of the library that holds all of these reference books.

Encyclopedias are arranged in alphabetical order and contain facts on people, places, things, events, and other topics. When you first begin looking up information on a subject the encyclopedia is a good place to go because it will give you a broad **overview** of the subject. Although an encyclopedia will probably give you the "who?," "what?," "where?," "when?," and "how?," it usually does not answer the "why?" or discuss both sides of a **controversial** topic. If you want to find out more than just general information about something, you should check books, magazines, newspapers, and other sources in *addition* to the encyclopedia.

THE ENCYCLOPEDIA INDEX

Often you will be able to go to the letter volume that corresponds with the first letter of your subject name. For example, if you wanted to find out more about Mexico, you could go to the "M" volume and look for "Mexico" alphabetically.

However, finding a topic is not always this easy. Sometimes you might look up your topic name and find nothing is listed. If you were interested specifically in Acapulco, a city in Mexico, you would probably not find it in the "A" encyclopedia. If, however, you looked up "Acapulco" in the encyclopedia index, you would see that information could be found in the "M" encyclopedia under "Mexico" — the index will also give you the exact page number that the city is discussed on.

The index is usually the last book or volume in an encyclopedia set and it will list all of the subjects that are covered in the entire set. Depending on what encyclopedia set you use, you will find that some indexes will give the volume *letter* and page(s) and some will give the volume *number* and page(s).

Look at the sample index entry below that lists the volume letters and pages.

Ships	
navigation	N-75
ocean liners (with pictures)	O-25
shipbuilding industry	S-155
submarines	S-452
Viking ships	V-331
whaling ships	W-158

If you wanted to learn more about ocean liners would you look under "T" for "transportation," or "S" for "ships?" Since you already know the type of transportation, you would look under "ships." You would also find the information you need on page 25 in the "O" volume. You can also see that there are pictures with this entry. An encyclopedia index will generally note if there are pictures, maps, or diagrams included in the entry you are looking up.

NAME _____

STUDYING ENCYCLOPEDIA INDEX

Study the entry for "**Leaf**" in each and then answer the questions.

BOOK OF KNOWLEDGE

Leaf [botany] L:151 *with pictures*
   Bud B:675 *with pictures*
   Deciduous Tree D:70
   Fern (Parts of a Fern) F:74 *with pictures*
   Grass (The Grass Plant) G:434
   Photosynthesis P:434
   Plant (Leaves) P:536 *with pictures*
   Transpiration T:379
   Tree T:410 (Leaves) T:417 *with diagrams*
   Vegetable (Leaves) V:310 *with pictures*

---

1. _____ Can you find a picture of the grass plant?

2. _____ On what pages can you find information about the leaves of trees?

3. _____ Would this encyclopedia be an excellent choice if you needed to include pictures in your report?

4. _____ Are vegetable leaves discussed in this encyclopedia? What volume and page number?

5. _____ On what pages can you find information about the leaf bud and leaf fern?

6. _____ You need to know about plant leaves. Can this encyclopedia help you?

7. _____ You need information about plants you can eat. Will this encyclopedia help you? What volume and page number?

8. _____ Will *Book of Knowledge* be a good choice for a picture report?

COMPARING
ENCYCLOPEDIA INDEXES

BOOK OF KNOWLEDGE

Leaf [botany] L:151 *with pictures*
    Bud B:675 *with pictures*
    Deciduous Tree D:70
    Fern (Parts of a Fern) F:74 *with pictures*
    Grass (The Grass Plant) G:434
    Photosynthesis P:434
    Plant (Leaves) P:536 *with pictures*
    Transpiration T:379
    Tree T:410 (Leaves) T:417 *with diagrams*
    Vegetable (Leaves) V:310 *with picturess*

LEAF	WORLD BOOK
Leaf with pictures	L 131
Bud with pictures	B 553
Fern with pictures	F 76
Grass (the grass plant)	G 314
Plant (leaves) with pictures	P 485
Tree (leaves)	T 334
Vegetable (leaves) with pictures	V 234

(Use this chart with page 67.)

NAME _____

THE ENCYCLOPEDIA INDEX

Study the entry for leaf in each of the encyclopedia indexes listed on page 66 and then answer the questions.

Answer the questions below. Remember you may have to check both indexes.

1. _____ Where would you look for a picture of a leaf in this index? One that you could eat?

2. _____ You need to know how to feed your plants. Where do you look?

3. _____ What happens to leaves in the fall and why?

4. _____ Do leaves ever become fossils?

5. _____ How do plants function (work)? Where do you look?

6. _____ Can you explain why leaves change colors? Where do you look?

7. _____ Are leaves important to trees? What volume do you check?

8. _____ How many pages in "trees and their leaves?"

9. _____ On what two pages can you find a picture?

10. _____ Which encyclopedia would give you more information about how plants work?

11. _____ Which one would give more information about what plants/leaves look like?

THE ENCYCLOPEDIA INDEX

Now look at an entry for *leaf* in another encyclopedia.

LEAVES, of plants	L 114-20
color change	L 117
feeding of plants	F 482
function of plants	P 293-94
how leaf fossils were formed	G 120
leaves we eat	P 307 picture P 306
trees and their leaves	T 275-78

Write your own entry for the entry LEAF:

_____

_____

_____

_____

_____

_____

_____

_____

_____

_____

_____

_____

COMPARING ENCYCLOPEDIA INDEXES

Each encyclopedia set is different. You will not find the same subjects in every encyclopedia set, nor will you find the same presentation of information in one set as you will in another.

Let's look at two different encyclopedia indexes on the same subject.

Animals	
Breeding	B-602
Fur	F-165
Pets	P-178-189
Wildlife	W-309
Zoos	Z-117
(Encyclopedia of Science)	

Animals	
Desert Animals	D-118
Extinct Animals	E-310
Farm Animals	F-308
Jungle Animals	J-284
Wildlife	W-609
(Encyclopedia of Arts and Science)	

What encyclopedia will help you find information about wildlife? Both encyclopedias will help you. What volume will help you in the *Encyclopedia of Science*? Check volume "W" on page 309. But check volume "W" on *page 609* in the *Encyclopedia of Arts and Science*.

Can you find information about pets in both indexes? No. You must look under volume "P" on page 178–179 in the *Encyclopedia of Science*.

Where can you find information about extinct animals? Check volume "E" on page 310 in the *Encyclopedia of Arts and Science*.

COMPARING ENCYCLOPEDIA INDEXES

<u>Dinosaurs</u>

Fossils	F-123–131
How dinosaurs found food	D-117–120
How dinosaurs lived	D-121–23
How and why dinosaurs disappeared	D-125–26
Poems about dinosaurs	P-107

Science Times Encyclopedia

<u>Dinosaurs</u>

Bones	B-124–129
Flying ancient animals (pictures)	F-138
Fossils (pictures)	F-37
Glaciers and dinosaurs	G-334–339
Prehistoric animals	P-111

Science World Encyclopedia

(Use with page 71.)

COMPARING ENCYCLOPEDIA INDEXES

Write the name of the encyclopedia, volume, and the page number that you would go to for information. *(Use the chart on page 70.)*

1. _____ You need information about weather conditions and the dinosaur. Did glaciers have any thing to do with the disappearance of the dinosaur?

2. _____ How did the dinosaurs disappear?

3. _____ Can you find a picture of dinosaur fossils?

4. _____ Did dinosaurs ever fly?

5. _____ Can you find any poems about dinosaurs?

6. _____ Can you find any information about the fossils of dinosaurs?

7. _____ What did dinosaurs eat?

8. _____ _____ Is there any information about the supersaurus?

9. _____ Is the dinosaur the largest prehistoric animal that ever lived?

10. _____ How are reptiles related to the dinosaur?

11. _____ Can you find any pictures of dinosaurs?

12. _____ How did the dinosaur live?

13. _____ Under what heading can you find information in both encyclopedias?

14. _____ You need to do much artwork for the cover of your dinosaur report. Which encyclopedia would be most helpful?

15. _____ You need much information about the type of animal the dinosaur was and how it lived. What encyclopedia would be most helpful?

USING HEADINGS

When you read an encyclopedia article, you may find that there is much information for you to read. If you are writing a report, this may take you much time. How can you find the headings? Encyclopedia headings can help you. They divide the article into parts. They work as book chapters do. You need not read an entire encyclopedia article to find information. Skim or read the headings. They will tell you what is in that part of the article.

For example, let's look at headings and subheadings for the article about the plants.

Plants

Importance of Plants   *heading*
food   *subheading*
medicines   *subheading*

Parts of Plants   *heading*
roots   *subheading*
stems   *subheading*
leaves   *subheading*
flowers   *subheading*

Plant Enemies   *heading*
diseases   *subheading*
pests   *subheading*

Subheadings are under headings. They are just an additional way of dividing the article. Let's say you need information about how a plant uses its parts. What headings do you need? What subheading will tell you about the stems? See *stems*. Let's say you are writing a report about the problems plants have with insects and other pests. What part of the article will help you? See the heading *Plant Enemies* and see the subheadings *diseases* and *pests*.

SUBHEADINGS

DINOSAURS

<u>Time of the Dinosaurs</u>
The Dinosaur and Where it Lived
Plant Life During Time of the Dinosaur
Animal Life During the Time of the Dinosaur
Land and Climate During the Time of the Dinosaur

<u>Kinds of Dinosaurs</u>
Large
Small
Flying

<u>How Dinosaurs Lived</u>
Getting Food
Protection Against Enemies

<u>Working with Dinosaur Fossils</u>
Finding Fossils
Digging Fossils
Fossils and Museums

(Use with page 74.)

ENCYCLOPEDIA HEADINGS

(Use with the chart on page 73.)

1. _____ You need information for your report about how fossils are displayed in museums. What subheading will help?

2. _____ Each member of your group will write a chapter about dinosaurs. Your topic is dinosaur bones and fossils. What heading will help?

3. _____ Did dinosaurs disappear because of their enemies? What subheading will help?

4. _____ Did dinosaurs ever eat tree leaves? What subheading will help?

5. _____ What were weather conditions like during the time of the dinosaur? What subheading will help?

6. _____ Did dinosaurs like any special type of area for their homes? What subheading will help?

7. _____ Did dinosaurs ever eat other animals? What subheading will help?

8. _____ How do scientists remove fossils from the earth? What subheading will help?

9. _____ Did dinosaurs ever fly? What subheading will help?

10. _____ What did the earth look like during dinosuar times? What subheading will help?

11. _____ What type of dinosaurs existed? What heading and three subheadings will help?

12. _____ What four subheadings and heading will help you learn what life was like during the times of the dinosaurs?

13. _____ What can you find out about dinosaurs and museums? What subheadings will help?

SUBHEADINGS

Encyclopedia Headings and Subheadings

KITES

<u>How Kites Fly</u>
<u>Types of Kites</u>
Flat Kite
Bowed Kite
Box Kite
Flying Kite
Triangular Kite

<u>History of the Kite</u>
Early Kites
In China
In Europe
In America

<u>Uses of Kites</u>
In government
In weather forecasting
In science experiments

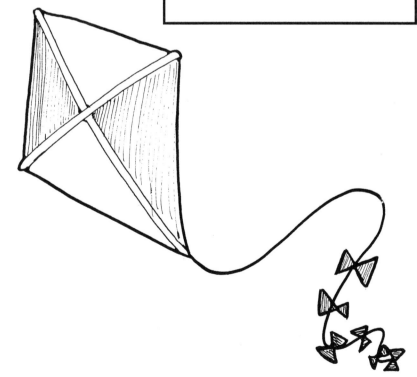

(Use with page 76.)

NAME _____

ENCYCLOPEDIA HEADINGS AND SUBHEADINGS

(Use with the chart on page 75.)

1. _____ Did the first kite to fly have a triangular shape? What subheading will help?

2. _____ Did the Chinese invent the kite? What subheading will help?

3. _____ You need to know how to build a kite so that it will fly. What heading will help?

4. _____ Were kites ever used by governments? What subheading will help?

5. _____ You plan to write a report about the kite in other countries. What heading will help you?

6. _____ How are kites used in America?

7. _____ Are kites ever used to predict what the weather will be like? What subheading will help?

8. _____ You plan to give a talk about the different kinds of kites. What heading will help?

9. _____ Are kites ever used in Europe? Name the subheading that will help.

10. _____ You plan a report about the types of kites and how to build them. What two headings will help?

    _____

11. _____ What heading will help you learn about how kites are helpful? What three subheadings will also help?

    _____

    _____

    _____

SEE ALSO REFERENCES

Let's say that you find the encyclopedia that you need. You find the page of the article you need. You read the article. But you could use more information. Where do you go? How do you find it? At the end of the encyclopedia article are a list of subjects. Not every article will have them. But, if they do, you will see the words, *See also.*

See also references tell you where you can find other encyclopedia articles. These articles are related to the subject of the article. For example, let's say you find POST OFFICE in the encyclopedia. At the end of the article you may see:

> See also: airmail; Pony Express; stamps; stamp
> collecting; zip code.

Let's say you need information about how the Pony Express began. You would look in the letter P volume under *Pony Express.* Let's say you have a cousin who collects stamps. You want to know more about the hobby. See also *stamp collecting.* And, let's say you want to know how air mail delivery works. You can see *post office* and see also *airmail.*

If you know how to use *see also references*, you can save time and energy in your searching for information. Let's look at some *see also references.*

SEE ALSO REFERENCES

1. *Pipe* See also organ; flute; trumpet.
2. *Pirate* See also Blackbeard; Captain Kidd; Sir Francis Drake
3. *Plants* See also plant diseases and pests; garden flowers; wild flowers; shrubs; vegetables.
4. *Pottery* See also ceramics (history); china (sculpture and pottery); pictures; Greece; ancient (pictures Indian); American (arts and crafts); prehistoric people (discoveries and inventions).
5. *Post Office* See also airmail; envelope; Pony Express; rural delivery; stamp; stamp collecting; zip code.
6. *Pearls* See also birthstone; button; gem (color picture); oyster.
7. *Parrot* See also Florida (places to visit with parrots); lovebird; macaw; parakeet.
8. *Painting* See also artists; stained glass; Indian (American) painting/crafts.

1. You plan on writing a report about the early ways of delivering the mail. Your report will discuss stamps, too. See post office and see also _____ and _____ .

2. You are drawing a cover for your report about birds. You plan to include a picture of a parrot. What kinds of parrots exist? See parrot and see also _____ and _____ and _____ .

3. You want to learn how to draw. You plan to use paints in your picture. See painting and see also _____ .

4. You are writing an extra credit report about pirates for your history class. See pirate and see also _____ and _____ and _____ .

5. Your music teacher has room for one more instrument in the band. It must be a pipe instrument. See pipe and see also _____ and _____ and _____ .

6. You are writing a report about famous artists. See painting and see also _____ .

7. You need a picture of wild flowers for your report cover. See plants and see also _____ .

8. You plan to write a report about the arts and crafts of the American Indian. See painting and see also _____ .

9. You plan to write a report about how mail is delivered across the country. See post office and see also _____ .

10. You plan to find out what birthstone you have. You think it is a pearl. See pearl and see also _____ .

SEE ALSO REFERENCES

1. *Magnet* See also compass; electricity.
2. *Magnifying glass* See also lens; microscope.
3. *Maps* See also chart; colonial life in America (map of the colonies).
4. *Globe* See also weather (making a weather map) World History picture of where early explorers traveled).
5. *Maple tree* See also maple syrup; tree (picture of North American maple tree).
6. *Marble* See also building stone (marble); limestone; rock (picture); sculpture (pictures).
7. *Mars* See also planet; solar system; space travel.
8. *Masks* See also Africa; Egypt; American Indian
9. *Memory* See also amnesia; brain (thinking and remembering); learning.
10. *Mercury* See also evening star; planet; solar system; space travel.

1. You need information about Mars. You need a picture of the planet and where it is in the solar system. See Mars and see also _____ and _____.

2. You plan a report about how students learn. See memory and see also _____.

3. Your teacher asked for volunteers to research how maple syrup is made. See maple tree and see also _____.

4. How does a magnet relate to electricity? See magnet and see also _____.

5. For extra credit you plan on writing about the American Indian. You plan on writing about their colorful masks. See masks and see also _____.

6. How do scientists make weather maps? See globe and see also _____.

7. Your science class is studying the magnifying glass and the microscope. How does the magnifying glass work inside the microscope? See magnifying glass and see also _____.

8. What do Egyptian masks look like? See masks and see also _____.

9. You need a map of the thirteen colonies for your history report. See maps and see also _____.

10. You are writing a science report about the planet Mercury. You need to know where it is in the solar system. See Mercury and see also _____.

SEE ALSO REFERENCES

1. *Airplane* See also airplane (models); helicopter; Wright Brothers; test pilots.
2. *Amphibian* See also frog; toad; salamander.
3. *Animals* See also nature study; pets; wildlife; zoos; protective coloring.
4. *Ant* See also anteater; insect; termite.
5. *Antennae* See also ant (sense); bee (body of the honey bee); insect (senses of insects); beetle (bodies of beetles); butterfly (the head).
6. *Apple* See also cider; fruit (chart of leading fruits); tree (picture).
7. *Astronaut* See also space travel; Cape Canaveral; Armstrong, Neal; Glenn, John.
8. *Astronomy* See also stars; constellation; galaxy; Halley's Comet; space travel.
9. *Atlas* See also maps (how they are made).
10. *Automobile* See also automobile industry (pictures); for (family); automobile, models (hobby).

1. You plan a report about space travel. Most of your report will be about the astronauts. See astronaut and see also _____ and _____ and _____ .
2. Your teacher started a unit on the stars. Where can you find more information about Halley's Comet? See stars and see also _____ and _____ .
3. Your report about animals needs more information. You plan to write about animals in the zoos. See animals and see also _____ .
4. You will write an extra credit report about how animals use their colors in the wild. See animals and see also _____ .
5. You volunteered to make cider for the class project. You know that you begin with apples. See apples and see also _____ .
6. Your cousin thinks cars are great. You plan to get a model kit for his birthday. But you need an idea of the different model cars. See automobile and see also _____ .
7. You think planes are great. You plan a report about the first people connected with the airplane. Who are they? See airplane and see also _____ .
8. You were looking at an atlas (book of maps). How are maps made? See atlas and see also _____ .
9. You need pictures of cars for your class. See automobile and see also _____ .
10. Your class is studying insects. The last chapter discussed how an antenna works. What information can you find about antennae? See_____ and see also _____ and_____ and _____ .

OVERVIEW USING THE ENCYCLOPEDIA INDEX

Look at the two following encyclopedia indexes. Then answer the following questions.

<u>Birds</u>

Birds (chart of the most common birds)	B-367
Blackbird	B-209
Crow (pictures of common types)	C-67
Duck (pictures of types of nests	D-308
Redwing Blackbird (song)	R.62
Robin	R-117
Sea gull	S-319

Encyclopedia of the World

<u>Birds</u>

Birds (descriptions of their songs)	B-407
Bluejay (description of their nest)	B-309
Cardinal (picture)	C-38
Mallard Duck	M-113
Sparrow	S-47
Whooping Crane	W-39

Encyclopedia of Knowledge

(Use with page 82.)

OVERVIEW—COMPARING ENCYCLOPEDIAS

Read each encyclopedia index found on page 81. Then answer these questions. Name the encyclopedia, volume, and page number for each question.

1. _____ Where do you look for information about the songs of birds?

2. _____ Is the spotted sparrow a common bird? Where can you find a list of the most common birds?

3. _____ Where can you find a picture of the nest of a duck?

4. _____ Where can you find information about the sea gull?

5. _____ Where can you find information about a sparrow?

6. _____ Where can you find information about the cardinal?

7. _____ Where can you find information about ducks?

8. _____ Where can you find information about birds' nests?

9. _____ Is there any information about the whooping crane?

10. _____ Birds' songs. Where can you find information about them?

NAME _____

ENCYCLOPEDIA INVESTIGATION

Choose a person you would like to find out more about. Find that person in the encyclopedia and answer the following questions:

1. Determine where and when he/she was born

2. Where he/she grew up

3. Why he/she is famous

4. When he/she died

5. Something about him/her you feel is important

I am studying about _____

_____

_____

_____

_____

_____

_____

_____

_____

Source of Information:

_____   _____
          Subject Name   Encyclopedia

_____   _____
      Volume   Pages

NAME _____

WHERE IN THE WORLD IS IT?

Select a country other than the United States or Canada and look it up in the encyclopedia. Go to a map or globe to help you choose.

Find out:

1. an important historical fact.
2. how many square miles this country has.
3. the population.
4. two chief products.
5. the currency (money).
6. the main language spoken.
7. places to visit.

Don't tell the name. Let your classmates guess.

_____

_____

_____

_____

_____

_____

_____

_____

_____

_____

Source of Information: _____

                                        Encyclopedia

_____   _____   _____
       Subject Name   Volume   Pages

COMPARING ENCYCLOPEDIAS

An ENCYCLOPEDIA is a book of facts about persons, places, things, and events, usually arranged in alphabetical order.

Choose two encyclopedias.
Call one ENCYCLOPEDIA A, and the other ENCYCLOPEDIA B.
Look up the topic COMET in each.
Make out the following report on the contents of each article.

ENCYCLOPEDIA A:

Name _____

Subject Name _____

Author of Article (if given) _____

Edition (year) _____ Volume _____ Pages _____

ENCYCLOPEDIA B:

Name _____

Subject Name _____

Author of Article (if given) _____

Edition (year) _____ Volume _____ Pages _____

Answer **YES** or **NO**

Is there a picture of a comet?   A _____ B _____

Is the pronunciation of the word "comet" given?   A _____ B _____

Are additional references suggested?   A _____ B _____

Answer briefly but completely the following questions:

What information about the comet is given in both ENCYCLOPEDIA A and ENCYCLOPEDIA B?

_____

_____

_____

_____

_____

What information is given in A but not in B? _____

_____

_____

_____

What information is given in B but not in A? _____

_____

_____

_____

In writing a report on the comet, you might use the encyclopedia articles for background information. Where might you find additional information?

_____

_____

_____

USING THE ENCYCLOPEDIA SPECIALIZED TYPES

Encyclopedias can give you much information for your report. But remember the well-know encyclopedias which you are probably familiar with are not the ONLY resources for information. Encyclopedias cover a wide range of topics. *Specialized encyclopedias* cover a wide range of information about one large topic. For example, you might check an encyclopedia of science for more information about science topics. First check the general encyclopedia before you check the specialized encyclopedia. This method will help you focus on what you need to find.

Next check the index of the specialized encyclopedia. These indexes work just like the general indexes do. Let's say you need information about black holes. Check under black holes. Are there any cross-references at the end of the article? Are there any names of scientists who talk about this subject? If so, check these names in the encyclopedia. Are there any related topics to black holes? If so, check these topics, too.

Remember specialized encyclopedias are an excellent resource to find concise information about a wide range of specialized topics. They can provide charts, tables, pictures, and diagrams for your report. Often they can shorten your research time by helping you focus upon the exact areas you need to check in other resources. A name. A place. A definition or another aspect of your topic may be discussed or briefly mentioned in the article that you may not have known existed! These are good resources. Use them!

USING THE SPECIALIZED ENCYCLOPEDIA

Read these report topics. What specialized encyclopedias might give you information?

> *The Encyclopedia of Invention*
> *The Encyclopedia of Hobbies*
> *The Collectibles Encyclopedia*
> *American Encyclopedia of History*
> *Science Encyclopedia of Today*
> *Art Today Encyclopedia*

1. black holes _____

2. Civil War _____

3. how the cotton gin works _____

4. Paul Revere's ride _____

5. early colonial times _____

6. abstract art _____

7. quasars _____

8. novas _____

9. Van Gogh and impressionism _____

10. candle making _____

11. stamp collections _____

12. whaling industry in early America _____

13. the automobile _____

14. sailing _____

15. sculpture _____

USING THE SPECIALIZED ENCYCLOPEDIA

Read these report topics. What specialized encyclopedias might give you information?

Encyclopedia of Sports	*Encyclopedia of Inventions*
Art in America	*Encyclopedia of Science*
Encyclopedia of World Art	*Space and Star Encyclopedia*
Encyclopedia of World History	*American Encyclopedia of History*
Hobby Master Encyclopedia	*The Collectibles Encyclopedia*

1. early explorers _____

2. landscape painters _____

3. latest discoveries _____

4. African history _____

5. history of soccer _____

6. movie pictures _____

7. satellites _____

8. Australian colonization _____

9. postcards _____

10. model airplanes _____

THE ATLAS

The atlas is a book of maps and facts about geography. Generally an atlas contains many different types of maps for all of the areas of the world. In order to use an atlas you should be familiar with some atlas vocabulary.

Legend (or Key)

The legend will help you read a map. It will tell you what the different colored areas of a map mean, as well as the *scale* or how many miles/kilometers are equal to one inch/centimeter on the map. You will find this measurement marked off on a small numbered line. Depending on the map you are using, the legend will also give you any other information you will need to know how to read the map.

Symbols

Symbols in an atlas stand for a condition or feature of the landscape. These symbols will show you human-made features (railroads, airports, etc.) as well as natural features (rivers, lakes, mountains, etc.). Usually symbols are included in the legend next to the map. (You may find the common symbols in a large legend at the beginning of the atlas.)

Index

To easily locate any place in the world (country, city, island, river, mountain, etc.) simply find the place name (alphabetically) in the index. The index will tell you exactly where in the atlas you will find the place you are looking for.

You should also know the definition of the following types of maps that are generally found in an atlas.

> **Relief Map**—shows the physical geography of a country—the mountains, rivers, lakes, plains, and deserts.
>
> **Political Map**—shows (by a color plan), nations, countries, state boundaries, and principal and capital cities.
>
> **Economic Map**—shows where products are grown and where various industries are (cattle, wheat, corn, etc.)

These are the three major types of maps; others include climate (temperatures, vegetation), population, transportation, precipitation (rainfall, snowfall), and time zones. Some atlases contain even more types of maps to show other detailed information about a country or area.

When looking for information on specific areas of the world, using an atlas is much easier than finding the same information in a book—and you will be surprised at how much you can learn by simply looking at maps!

USING AN ATLAS

Turn to the index in an atlas and find the pages listed under "Australia." In order to answer the following questions you will need to find the *legend* (or *key*) for the different maps of Australia. The legend will help you read each map. Answer the following questions:

1. How much precipitation does the central area of Australia receive yearly?

   _____

2. How many areas of Australia are uninhabited (unpopulated)?

   _____

3. The largest area of Australia is used for _____ .
   (Hint: Use the economic/mineral map.)

4. How many time zones does Australia have? _____

5. Using the climate (environment) map, describe the large center area of Australia. _____

6. Name two oceans that surround Australia. _____ and

   _____

7. On which side of Australia is the Great Barrier Reef located? (North, South, East, or West) _____

8. Name three seas that surround Australia. _____ ,

   _____ , and _____

9. The northeast section of Australia is called _____ .

10. What is the name of the island state off the southern coast of Australia?

    _____

MAPPING

Look under "Africa" in an atlas and label three rivers, five major cities, the surrounding bodies of water.

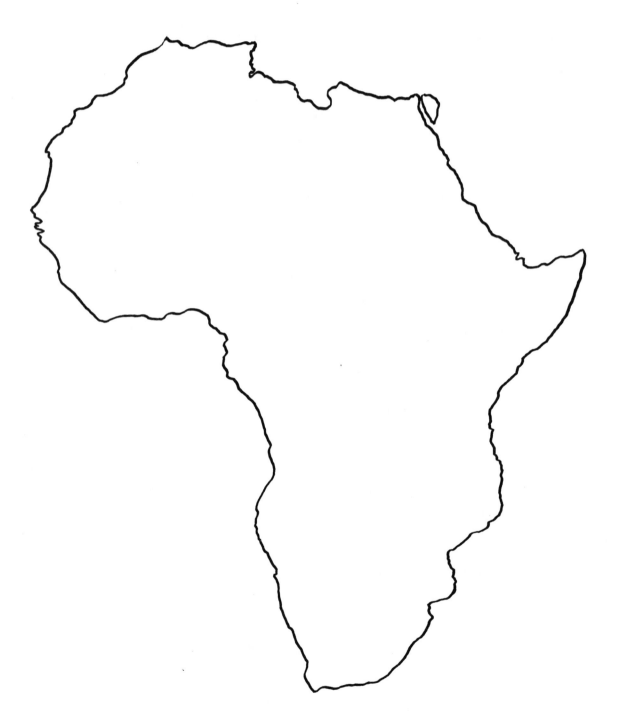

ATLAS

An atlas is a book of maps and related geographical facts. An atlas often contains several kinds of maps for one area. Each map may give information about one feature of the area, such as rainfall, temperature, or natural resources.

To locate the place you are looking for you must use the index.

Directions: Below is a sample index from Goode's World Atlas. Use the index to answer the questions.

Fairhaven, Ma. (far- ha ven)........... 111	41.35N	70.55W
Fairhaven, Md. ....56 d	38.47N	77.05W
Fair Haven, Vt. 111	43.35N	73.15W
Fair I., Scot. (far)............................162 a	59.34N	1.41W
Fair Lawn, NJ 55	40.56N	74.07W
Fairlee, Md. ....56 d	38.52N	77.16W
Fairmont, Mn. (far mont) 115	43.39N	94.26W
Fairmont, WV.................................. 111	39.30N	80.10W
Fairmont City, Il............................. 119 e	38.39N	90.95W
Fairmount, In. 110	40.25N	85.45W
Fairmount, Ks. ....56 d	38.54N	76.55W
Fair Oaks, Ga. (far oks) .... 112 c	33.56N	84.33W
Fairport, NY (far port) 111	43.05N	77.30W
Fairport Harbor, Oh. 110	41.45N	81.15W
Fairseat, Eng. 62	51.30N	0.20E
Fairview, NJ 55	40.49N	74.00W
Fairview, Ok. (far vu) 122	36.16N	98.28W
Fairview, Or. ....118 c	45.32N	112.26W
Fairview, Ut.....................................121	39.35N	111.30W

1. In what state would you find Fairmont City? _____

2. On what page would you find Fair Haven? _____

3. What is the latitude for Fairport Harbor? _____ N

4. What is the longitude for Fairport Harbor ?_____ W

5. Write the pronunciation for Fairview _____

6. In how many different states could you find a city called Fairview? _____

Goode's World Atlas. Seventeenth ed. Rand McNally. Chicago. 1986 p. 282

NAME _____

EXAMINING THE ATLAS

Select an ATLAS from your classroom or from the library and complete the following questions while carefully examining the ATLAS.

Author (or editor) _____

Title _____

Publisher _____

Place of Publication _____

Copyright Date _____

Call Number _____

What kinds of maps does this ATLAS contain? _____

_____

_____

_____

_____

Does this ATLAS have an index? _____

Does each map have a legend? _____

Is there a legend in the front of the atlas? _____

THE
BIOGRAPHICAL DICTIONARY

You have probably noticed that at the back of most dictionaries there is a section of biographical entries—although these are helpful to check the spelling of a person's name or to verify a birth or death date, this type of format will not give you much more information about the person you are checking. If you want a broader overview about a specific person that is quick and easy to find, the biographical dictionary is a place to look.

A *biographical dictionary* is a special kind of dictionary—it is a dictionary of people. This resource is a helpful reference tool to get you started on a project or a report. When you have no information on a person, the biographical dictionary will give you a starting place so that you can look to books on history, science, art, music, etc., to find more detailed information on how the person fit into his or her field and time period.

The names in a biographical dictionary are arranged alphabetically by last name. You will find each person's birth and death dates, nationality, primary reasons for importance, as well as contributions to society (i.e., an artist's major works, etc.).

NAME _____

USING THE BIOGRAPHICAL DICTIONARY

Using a biographical dictionary, locate the following information:

1. _____ What piece of writing is Miguel de Cervantes most famous for?

2. _____ When did Napoleon Bonaparte die?

3. _____ What newspaper did Ida B. Wells help start?

4. _____ What was the occupation of Zheng He?

5. _____ When was Martin Luther born?

6. _____ What song is Julia Ward Howe famous for writing?

7. _____ What were three of George Washington Carver's occupations?

_____

_____

8. _____ What nationality was Filippo Brunelleschi?

9. _____ Write the pronunciation for René Descartes.

10. _____ What is Jane Addams known for?

11. _____ What was the occupation of Anton van Leeuwenhoek?

12. _____ When was Leonardo da Vinci born?

13. _____ What nationality was Shogun Hirodata?

14. _____ List two of Eugene O'Neill's plays.

_____

15. _____ When did Harriet Tubman die?

WEBSTER'S NEW BIOGRAPHICAL DICTIONARY

Webster's Biographical Dictionary is an alphabetical list of famous people. These people represent various historical periods, nationalities, races, religions, and occupations. Each entry contains information on syllable division and pronunciation.

Directions: Below is a sample from Webster's Biographical Dictionary. Use it to answer the following questions.

> **Buchanan**, Sir George. 1831-1895. English physician and exponent of sanitary science. Chief agent in eradicating typhus fever, reducing mortality from tuberculosis, and controlling cholera. His eldest son, Sir George Seaton (1869-1936), hygienist, was senior medical officer, Ministry of Health (1919-34).
>
> **Buchanan**, Sir George Cunningham. 1865-1940. British civil engineer, specialist in harbor, dock, and river works.
>
> **Buchanan**, Sir George William. 1854-1924. British diplomatist of Scottish family; ambassador at St. Petersburg (1910-18).
>
> **Buchanan**, James. 1791-1868. Fifteenth president of the United States, b. near Mercersburg, Pa. Grad. Dickinson College (1809). Adm. to bar, Lancaster, Pa. (1812); volunteer in the War of 1812; member, U.S. House of Representatives (1821-31). U.S. minister to Russia (1834-34). U.S. senator (1834-45). Secretary of state (1845-49). U.S. minister to Great Britain (1853-56). President of the United States (1857-61) during years just preceding Civil War; failed to meet challenge of South Carolina's secession (Dec. 20, 1860), and endeavored to avoid the issue of civil conflict.

1. For what was James Buchanan famous? _____

   _____

2. From what country is Sir George William Buchanan? _____

3. When did George Cunningham Buchanan die? _____

4. What occupation did Sir George Buchanan have? _____

5. Where was James Buchanan born? _____

Webster's Biographical Dictionary. G. & G. Merriam Company. Springfield, Massachusetts. 1976 p. 208

WEBSTER'S NEW
BIOGRAPHICAL DICTIONARY

Choose a person's name you know very little about.

_____

Name

Give the dates of the person's life.

_____   _____
Birth   Death

Write some information about the person including what the person is known best for doing. Write at least five facts.

_____

_____

_____

_____

_____

_____

_____

_____

_____

_____

_____

_____

_____

WEBSTER'S BIOGRAPHICAL DICTIONARY:

Famous Person	Nationality	Living or Dead	Profession
1. Albert Bernhard Nobel	_____	_____	_____
2. Carl Sandburg	_____	_____	_____
3. Henry Ford	_____	_____	_____
4. George Grenfell	_____	_____	_____
5. Byron R. White	_____	_____	_____
6. Greta Garbo	_____	_____	_____
7. Marc Chagall	_____	_____	_____
8. Henrik Ibsen	_____	_____	_____
9. Mary Wollstonecraft Shelley	_____	_____	_____
10. Pindar	_____	_____	_____

A SPECIAL KIND
OF BIOGRAPHICAL DICTIONARY

The *Junior Book of Authors* and the *Book of Junior Authors and Illustrators* series are a special kind of biographical dictionary. These books include information only about authors and illustrators of books for boys and girls.

Study the article about *Cynthia Rylant* and answer the following questions.

1. How did Cynthia Rylant first become interested in reading? _____

   _____

   _____

2. What was her first collection of stories called? _____

   _____

   _____

3. Why do you think her books have been so successful? _____

   _____

   _____

4. Where does she get most of her ideas for writing her books? _____

   _____

5. Where was Cynthia Rylant born? _____

6. What three colleges did she attend as a student? _____

   _____

7. Name two of her books that have been Caldecott Honor Books:

   _____

8. Why do you think her books will be enjoyed by boys and girls for many years
   to come? _____

   _____

JUNIOR BOOK OF AUTHORS
THIRD JUNIOR BOOK OF AUTHORS
FOURTH JUNIOR BOOK OF AUTHORS

Directions: Choose a favorite author. Find an autobiographical sketch of that author by using the index in the Third Junior Book of Authors or by looking for the last name at the top of the pages in all books. Write some information about the author.

Author's name _____

Author's dates: Born _____ Died _____

Author's books _____

_____

_____

Interesting facts about the author's life (at least five).

_____

_____

_____

_____

If you have read one of the author's books, write a brief book review.

Title of the book _____

Comments _____

_____

NAME _____

USING REFERENCE BOOKS: REVIEW

A. ENCYCLOPEDIA
B. DICTIONARY
C. *WORLD ALMANAC*
D. ATLAS
E. *JUNIOR BOOK OF AUTHORS*

In which of the above reference books would you look first to locate the following kinds of information? Place the letter symbol for the reference book you would use to find the information on the line provided.

_____ 1. Facts and statistics about a country.

_____ 2. Charts giving birth and death dates of important people.

_____ 3. Correct usage of a word.

_____ 4. Factual description of a country.

_____ 5. Events and progress of the previous year.

_____ 6. Location of cities, states, rivers.

_____ 7. Political boundaries.

_____ 8. The plural form of a word.

_____ 9. Information about writers and illustrators of children's stories.

_____ 10. Synonyms and antonyms.

_____ 11. Pictures of Presidents of the United States.

_____ 12. The voting statistics for the previous year.

_____ 13. Background information for a report.

_____ 14. All problems dealing with words.

_____ 15. Up-to-date sports records.

In what reference book in your library would you find a description of the departments of your state's government and the constitution for your state?

_____

WRITING A BOOK REPORT

Writing a book report is not only a good way of showing your teacher that you read and understood the book you chose, a book report can also inform your friends and classmates about a book *they* should read.

Here are some tips for writing a book report:

1. First state the title, the author, and the year the book was published. (If the book has pictures, name the illustrator as well.)

2. Next, state why you think the book is worthwhile or not worthwhile. Be careful not to use words like "good," "great," or "interesting." You friends would rather hear, if it was;

funny?	biographical?	sad?	inspiring?
scary?	historical?	suspenseful?	amusing?
lifelike?	imaginary?	romantic?	scientific?

   These are just a few questions you should consider when you are writing about a book. By choosing your words carefully, you can say much about a book in just one sentence. If you have difficulty thinking of ways to describe your book, you might want to use a thesaurus for help.

3. After talking about your book in a general sense, write a little about the most exciting part of the book—*but don't tell everything*. Remember, if you liked the book, you want to get others to read it. If you tell about all the exciting parts, no one will need to read it.

4. As you write your report be careful that you don't just retell the story. As point #3 suggests, tell a little about an exciting part to get your audience interested, but remember that your primary goal should be telling your friends *why* they should (or should not) read the book.

5. At the end of your report, write a short paragraph on the author (and/or illustrator). This will let your audience know something about the author's background and how this may have been a basis for the story or the author's style of writing.

Most libraries have books on the lives of children's authors and illustrators, otherwise a general encyclopedia often will have this information as well—ask your librarian.

NAME _____

WRITING A BOOK REPORT

Think of the last book you read. Write five informative sentences about it.

Title: _____   Author: _____

1. _____

2. _____

3. _____

4. _____

5. _____

Pick one of your favorite authors. Talk to your librarian and see if you have *The Book of Junior Authors and Illustrators* series in your library. (If not, check the encyclopedia or a biographical dictionary.) Write a short paragraph on the author you choose in the space below.

_____

_____

_____

_____

_____

_____

_____

_____

Find a "visual" for your book report. This might be a family tree, a time line explaining when the story took place, or a portrait of all the characters (or the most important characters) in the book. Label the characters to help you remember who they are.

THE NEWBERY AWARD

It is fitting that John Newbery's name should become a memorial in the field of children's literature. It was he who first saw the need for books to entertain and please children without any attempt to improve or instruct. He wanted to make children's books attractive. He set up displays of children's books expressly to attract children. Not only did he persuade others to write for children, but it is believed that he also wrote some of the books that he published. In London, his little book store at 65 Saint Paul's Churchyard displayed in the window the arresting notice, "Juvenile Library." Although his *Pretty Little Pocket Book*, *History of Little Goody Two-Shoes*, and his other publications for children survive now only as collector's pieces, his achievement is undeniable. He established children's book publishing as an important part of the book trade.

Frederic G. Melcher was like John Newbery in many ways. As Secretary of the American Booksellers Association, in 1919 he organized a nationwide observance of Children's Book Week, which had first been planned by Franklin Mathiews of the Boy Scouts of America before World War I. Since then, books for children have made a steady climb upward. In June 1921 Mr. Melcher made his historic plea for emphasis on excellence in children's literature at the meeting of the Children's Librarian's Selection of the American Library Association. It was his suggestion that a medal be given annually as an award to the author of the most distinguished contribution to American literature for children and that it be named for John Newbery, the renowned London book publisher of the eighteenth century. Mr. Melcher agreed to provide a bronze medal, engraved with the winner's name and the year of the award to deliver to the authorities of the American Library Association. All arrangements, and the methods and practice of selecting each annual winner was left entirely to the American Library Association. His suggestion was approved by the Association, and every year since then the John Newbery Medal has been presented to the author of the most distinguished contribution to American literature for children published the preceding year. One of the requirements is that the author be either a citizen or a resident of the United States. Each year during his lifetime, Mr. Melcher provided the medal, which was designed by the sculptor, Rene Chambellan. Since the death of Frederic Melcher on March 9, 1963, the donor of the medal has been his son, Daniel Melcher, who followed his father in the publishing business.

NEWBERY WINNERS and HONOR BOOKS

1922-*The Story of Mankind*
    by Willem Van Loon
        Honor Books:
The Great Quest. Charles Hawes
Cedric the Forester. Bernard Marshall
The Old Tabacco Shop. William Bowen
The Golen Fleece and the Heroes Who Lived
    Before Achilles. Padraic Colum
Windy Hill. Cornelia Meigs

1923-*The Voyages of Doctor Dolittle*
    by Hugh Lofting
        Honor Books:
No record

1924-*The Dark Frigate*
    by Charles B. Hawes
        Honor Books:
No record

1925-*Tales From Silver Lands*
    by Charles Finger
        Honor Books:
Nicholas. Anne Carroll Moore
Dream Coach. Anne Parrish

1926-*Shen of the Sea*
    by Arthur Bowie Chrisman
        Honor Books:
Voyagers. Padraic Colum

1927-*Smoky, the Cowhorse*
    by Will James
        Honor Books:
No record

1928-*Gay-Neck, the Story of a Pigeon*
    by Dhan Gopal Mukerji
        Honor Books:
The Wonder Smith and His Son. Ella Young
Downright Dencey. Caroline Snedeker

1929-*The Trumpeter of Krakow*
    by Eric P. Kelly
        Honor Books:
Pigtail of Ah Lee Ben Loo. John Bennett
Millions of Cats. Wanda Gag.
The Boy Who Was. Grace Hallock
Clearing Weather. Cornelia Meigs
Tod of the Fens. Elinor Whitney

1930-*Hitty, Her First Hundred Years*
    by Rachel Field
        Honor Books:
Daughter of the Seine. Jeanette Eaton
Pran of Albania. Elizabeth Miller
Jumping-Off Place. Marian Hurd McNeely
Tangle-Coated Horse and Other Tales.
    Ella Young.
Vaino. Julia Davis Adams
Little Blacknose. Hildegarde Swift.

1931-*The Cat Who Went to Heaven*
    by Elizabeth Coatsworth
        Honor Books:
Floating Island. Anne Parrish
The Dark Star of Itza. Alida Malkus
Queer Person. Ralph Hubbard
Mountains Are Free. Julia Davis Adams
Spice and the Devil's Cave. Agnes Hewes
Meggy MacIntosh. Elizabeth Gray Vining
Garram the Hunter. Herbert Best
Ood-le-uk the Wanderer. Alice Lide and
    Margaret Johansen

1932-*Waterless Mountain*
    by Laura A. Armer
        Honor Books:
The Fairy Circus. Dorothy Athrop
Calico Bush. Rachel Field
Boy of the South Seas. Eunice Tietjens
Truce of the Wolf and Other Tales of Old
    Italy. Mary Gould Davis

1933-*Young Fu of the Upper Yangtze*
    by Elizabeth Lewis
        Honor Books:
Swift Rivers. Cornelia Meigs.
The Railroad to Freedom. Hildegard Swift
Children of the Soil. Nora Burglon

1934-*Invincible Louisa*
    by Cornelia Meigs
        Honor Books:
The Forgotten Daughter. Caroline Snedeker
Swords of Steel. Elsie Singmaster
ABC Bunny. Wanda Gag
Winged Girl of Knossos. Erick Berry, pseud.
    (Allen Best)
New Land. Sarah Schmidt
Big Tree of Bunlahy. Padraic Colum
Glory of the Seas. Agnes Hewes
Apprentice of Florence. Anne Kyle

1935-*Dobry*
> by Monica Shannon
>> Honor Books:
>> *Pageant of Chinese History*. Elizabeth Seeger
>> *Davy Crockett*. Constance Rourke
>> *Day on Skates*. Hilda Van Stockum

1936-*Caddie Woodlawn*
> by Carol Brink
>> Honor Books:
>> *Honk: The Moose*. Phil Strong
>> *The Good Master*. Kate Serdy
>> *Young Walter Scott*. Elizabeth Gray Vining
>> *All Sail Set*. Armstrong Sperry

1937-*Roller Skates*
> by Ruth Sawyer
>> Honor Books:
>> *Phebe Fairchild: Her Book*. Lois Lenski
>> *Whistler's Van*. Idwal Jones
>> *Golden Basket*. Ludwig Bemelmans
>> *Winterbound*. Magery Bianco
>> *Audubon*. Constance Rourke
>> *The Codfish Market*. Agnes Hewes

1938-*The White Stag*
> by Kate Deredy
>> Honor Books:
>> *Pecos Bill*. James Cloyd Bowman
>> *Bright Island*. Mabel Robinson
>> *On the Banks of Plum Creek*. Laura Ingalls Wilder

1939-*Thimble Summer*
> by Elizabeth Enright
>> Honor Books:
>> *Nino*. Valenti Angelo
>> *Mr. Popper's Penguins*. Richard and Florence Atwater
>> *"Hello the Boat!"* Phyllis Crawford
>> *Leader by Destiny: George Washington, Man and Patriot*. Jeanette Eaton

1940-*Daniel Boone*
> by James Daugherty
>> Honor Books:
>> *The Singing Tree*. Kate Seredy
>> *Runner of the Mountain Tops*. Mabel Robinson
>> *By the Shores of Silver Lake*. Laura Ingalls Wilder
>> *Boy With a Pack*. Stephen W. Meader

1941-*Call It Courage*
> by Armstrong Sperry
>> Honor Books:
>> *Blue Willow*. Doris Gates
>> *Young Mac of Fort Vancouver*. Mary Jane Carr
>> *The Long Winter*. Laura Ingalls Wilder
>> *Nansen*. Anna Gertrude Hall

1942-*The Matchlock Gun*
> by Walter D. Edmonds
>> Honor Books:
>> *Little Town on the Prairie*. Laura Ingalls Wilder
>> *George Washington's World*. Genevieve Foster
>> *Indian Captive: The Story of Mary Jemison*. Lois Lenski
>> *Down Ryton Water*. Eva Roe Gaggin

1943-*Adam of the Road*
> by Elizabeth Gray Vining
>> Honor Books:
>> *The Middle Moffat*. Eleanor Estes
>> *"Have You Seen Tom Thumb?"* Mabel Leigh Hunt

1944-*Johnny Tremain*
> by Esther Forbes
>> Honor Books:
>> *These Happy Golden Years*. Laura Ingalls Wilder
>> *Fog Magic*. Julia Sauer
>> *Rufus M.* Eleanor Estes
>> *Mountain Born*. Elizabeth Yates

1945-*Rabbit Hill*
> by Robert Lawson
>> Honor Books:
>> *The Hundred Dresses*. Eleanor Estes
>> *The Silver Pencil*. Alice Dalgliesh
>> *Abraham Lincoln's World*. Genevieve Foster
>> *Lone Journey; the Life of Roger Williams*. Jeanette Eaton

1946-*Strawberry Girl*
> by Lois Lenski
>> Honor Books:
>> *Justin Morgan Had a Horse*. Marguerite Henry
>> *The Moved Outers*. Florence Crannell Means.
>> *Bhimsa, the Dancing Bear*. Christine Weston
>> *New Found World*. Katherine Shippen.

1947-*Miss Hickory*
    by Caroline S. Bailey
        Honor Books:
    Wonderful Year. Nancy Barnes
    Big Tree. Mary and Conrad Buff
    The Heavenly Tenants. William Maxwell
    The Avion My Uncle Flew. Cyrus Fisher
    The Hidden Treasure of Glaston. Eleanore
        Jewett

1948-*The Twenty-One Balloons*
    by William Pene de Bois
        Honor Books:
    Pancakes – Paris. Claire Huchet Bishop
    LiLun, Lad of Courage. Carolyn Treffinger
    *The Quaint and Curious Quest of Johnny
        Longfoot.* Catherine Besterman
    *The Cow-Tail Switch, and Other West
        African Stories.* Harold Courlander
    Misty of Chincoteague. Marguerite Henry

1949-*King of the Wind*
    by Marguerite Henry
        Honor Books:
    Seabird. Holling C. Holling
    Daughter of the Mountain. Louise Rankin
    My Father's Dragon. Ruth Gannett
    Story of the Negro. Arna Bontemps

1950-*The Door in the Wall*
    by Marguerite de Angeli
        Honor Books:
    Tree of Freedom. Rebecca Caudill
    The Blue Cat of Castle Town. Catherine
        Coblentz
    Kildee House. Rutherford Montgomery
    George Washington. Genevieve Foster
    Song of the Pines. Walter and Marion
        Havighurst

1951-*Amos Fortune, Free Man*
    by Elizabeth Yates
        Honor Books:
    Better Known as Johnny Appleseed. Mabel
        Leigh Hunt
    Gandhi, Fighter Without a Sword. Jeanette
        Eaton
    Abraham Lincoln, Friend of the People.
        Clara Ingram Judson
    The Story of Appleby Capple. Anne Parrish

1952-*Ginger Pye*
    by Eleanor Estes
        Honor Books:
    Americans Before Columbus. Elizabeth
        Baity
    Minn of the Mississippi. Holling C. Holling
    The Defender. Nicholas Kalashnikoff
    The Light at Tern Rock. Julia Sauer
    The Apple and the Arrow. Mary and Conrad
        Buff

1953-*Secret of the Andes*
    by Ann Nolan Clark
        Honor Books:
    Charlotte's Web. E.B. White
    Moccasin Trail. Eloise McGraw
    Red Sails to Capri. Anne Weil
    The Bears of Hemlock Mountain. Alice
        Dalgliesh
    Birthdays of Freedom v. I. Genevieve Foster

1954-*. . . And Now Miguel*
    by Joseph Krumgold
        Honor Books:
    All Alone. Claire Huchet Bishop
    Shadrach. Meindert de Jong
    Hurry Home Candy. Meindert de Jong
    Thedore Roosevelt, Fighting Patriot. Clara I.
        Judson

    Magic Maize. Mary and Conrad Buff
1955-*The Wheel on the School*
    by Meindert de Jong
        Honor Books:
    Courage of Sarah Noble. Alice Dalgliesh
    Banner in the Sky. James Ullman

1956-*Carry on Mr. Bowditch*
    by Jean Lee Latham
        Honor Books:
    The Secret River. Marjorie Kinnan Rawlings
    The Golden Name Day. Jennie Lindquist
    Men, Microscopes, and Living Things.
        Katherine Shippen

1957-*Miracles on Maple Hill*
    by Virginia Sorensen
        Honor Books:
    Old Yeller. Fred Gipson
    The House of Sixty Fathers. Meindert de
        Jong
    Mr. Justice Holmes. Clara I. Judson
    The Corn Grows Ripe. Dorothy Rhoads
    Black Fox of Lorne. Marguerite de Angeli

1958-*Rifles for Watie*
by Harold Keith
Honor Books:
The Horsecatcher. Mari Sandoz
Gone-Away Lake. Elizabeth Enright
The Great Wheel. Robert Lawson
Tom Paine, Freedom's Apostle. Leo Gurko

1959-*The Witch of Blackbird Pond*
by Elizabeth George Speare
Honor Books:
The Family Under The Bridge. Natalie S.
Carlson
Along Came a Dog. Meindert de Jong
Chucaro: Wild Pony of the Pampa. Francis
Kalnay
The Perilous Road. William O. Steel

1960-*Onion John*
by Joseph Krumgold
Honor Books:
My Side of the Mountain. Jean George
America is Born. Gerald W. Johnson
The Gammage Cup. Carol Kendall

1961-*Island of the Blue Dolphins*
by Scott O'Dell
Honor Books:
America Moves Forward. Gerald W.
Johnson
Old Ramon. Jack Schaeffer
Cricket in Times Square. George Selden,
pseud. (George Thompson)

1962-*The Bronze Bow*
by Elizabeth George Speare
Honor Books:
Frontier Living. Edwin Tunis
The Golden Goblet. Eloise Jarvis
Belling the Tiger. Mary Stolz

1963-*A Wrinkle in Time*
by Madeleine L'Engle
Honor Books:
*Thistle and Thyme; Tales and Legends from
Scotland.* Sorche Nic Leodhas, pseud.
(Leclaire Alger)
Men of Athens. Olivia Coolidge

1964-*It's Like This, Cat*
by Emily Neville
Honor Books:
Rascal. Sterling North
The Loner. Ester Wier

1965-*Shadow of a Bull*
by Maia Wojciechowska
Honor Books:
Across Five Aprils. Irene Hunt

1966-*I, Juan De Pare*
by Elizabeth Borton de Trevino
Honor Books:
The Black Cauldron. Lloyd Alexander
The Animal Family. Randall Jarrell
The Noonday Friends. Mary Stolz

1967-*Up a Road Slowly*
by Irene Hunt
Honor Books:
The Jazz man. Mary H. Weik
The King's Fifth. Scott O'Dell
Zalatah the Goat and Other Stories. Isaac
Bashevis

**1968-*From the Mixed-Up Files of Mrs.
Basil E. Frankweiler***
by E. L. Koingsburg
Honor Books:
*Jennifer, Hecate, Macbeth, William
McKinley, and Me, Elizabeth.* E.L.
Koingsburg
The Black Pearl. Scott O'Dell
The Egypt Game. Zilpha K. Snyder
The Fearsome Inn. Isaac Bashevis Singer

1969-*The High King*
by Lloyd Alexander
Honor Books:
To Be a Slave. Julius Lester
*When Shlemiel Went to Warsaw and Other
Stories.* Isaac Bashevis Singer

1970-*Sounder*
by William H. Armstrong
Honor Books:
Journey Outside. Mary Q. Steele
Our Eddie. Sulamith Ish-Kishor
*The Many Faces of Seing: An Introduction
to the Pleasure of Art.* Janet G. Moore

1971-*Summer of the Swans*
by Betsy Byars
Honor Books:
Enchantress from the Stars. Sylvia L.
Engdahl
Kneelknock Rise. Natalie Babbit
Sing Down the Moon. Scott O'Dell

1972-*Mrs. Frisby and the Rats of Nimh*
   by Robert C. O'Brien
     Honor Books:
Annie and the Old One. Miska Miles
Incident at Hawk's Hill. Allan W. Eckert
The Headless Cupid. Zilpha K. Snyder
The Planet of Junior Brown. Virginia
   Hamilton
The Tombs of Atuan. Ursula K. LeGuin

1973-*Julie of the Wolves*
   by Jean Craighead
     Honor Books:
Frog and Toad Together. Arnold Lobel
The Upstairs Room. Johanna Reiss
The Witches of Worm. Zilpha K. Synder

1974-*The Slave Dancer*
   by Paula Fox
     Honor Books:
The Dark is Rising. Susan Cooper

1975-*M. C. Higgins the Great*
   by Virginia Hamilton
     Honor Books:
Figgs and Phantoms. Ellen Raskin
My Brother Sam is Dead. James L. Collier
   and Christopher Collier
Phillip Hall Likes Me, I Reckon Maybe.
   Bette Greene
The Perilous Gard. Elizabeth Marie Pope

1976-*The Grey King*
   by Susan Cooper
     Honor Books:
Dragonwings. Laurence Yep
The Hundred Penny Box. Sharon Bell
   Mathis

1977-*Roll of Thunder, Hear My Cry*
   by Mildred D. Taylor
     Honor Books:
Abel's Island. William Steig
A String in the Harp. Nancy Bond.

1978-*Bridge to Terabithia*
   by Katherine Paterson
     Honor Books:
Anpao: An American Indian Odyssey.
   Jamake Highwater
Romona and Her Father. Beverly Cleary

1979-*The Westing Game*
   by Ellen Raskin
     Honor Books:
The Great Gilly Hopkins. Katherine
   Paterson

**1980-*A Gathering of Days: A New England
     Girl's Journal 1830-32***
   by Joan W. Blos
     Honor Books:
*The Road From Home: The Story of an
   Armenian Girl.* David Kherdian

1981-*Jacob Have I Loved*
   by Katherine Paterson
     Honor Books:
The Fledgling. Jane Langton
A Ring of Endless Light. Madeleine L'Engle

1982-*A Visit to William Blake's Inn*
   by Nancy Willard
     Honor Books:
Ramona Quinby, Age 8. Beverly Cleary
*Upon the Head of the Goat: A Childhood in
   Hungary, 1939-1944.* Aranka Siegal

1983-*Dicey's Song*
   by Cynthia Voigt
     Honor Books:
The Blue Sword. Robin McKinley
Dr. De Soto. William Steig
Graven Images. Paul Fleishman
Homesick: My Own Story. Jean Fritz
Sweet Whispers, Brother Rush. Virginia
   Hamilton

1984-*Dear Mr. Henshaw*
   by Beverly Cleary
     Honor Books:
The Sing of the Beaver. Elizabeth George
   Speare
A Solitary Blue. Cynthia Voigt
Sugaring Time. Katherine Lasky
The Wish Giver. Bill Brittain

1985-*The Hero and the Crown*
   by Patricia McKinley
     Honor Books:
Like Jake and Me. Mavis Jukes
The Moves Make the Man. Bruce Brooks
One-Eyed Cat. Paula Fox

1986-*Sarah, Plain and Tall*
  by Patricia MacLachlan
      Honor Books:
  *Commodore Perry in the Land of the
      Shogun.* Rhoda Blumberg
  Dogsong. Gary Paulsen

1987-*The Whipping Boy*
  by Sid Fleischman
      Honor Books:
  A Fine White Dust. Cynthia Rylant
  On My Honor. Marion Dane Bauer
  *Volcano: The Eruption and Healing of
      Mount St. Helens.* Patricia Lauber

1988-*Lincoln: A Photobiography*
  by Russell Freedman
      Honor Books:
  After The Rain. Norma Fox Mazer
  Hatchet. Gary Paulsen

1989-*Joyful Noise: Poems for Two Voices*
  by Paul Fleischman
      Honor Books:
  *In The Beginning: Creation Stories from
      Around the World.* Virginia Hamilton

1990-*Number the Stars*
  by Lois Lowry
      Honor Books:
  Afternoon of the Elves. Janet Taylor Lisle
  Shabanu: Daughter of the Wind. Suzanne
      Fisher Staples
  The Winter Room. Gary Paulsen

1991-*Maniac Magee*
  by Jerry Spinelli
      Honor Books:
  The True Confessions of Charlotte Doyle.
      Avi

1992-*Shiloh*
  by Phyllis Reynolds
      Honor Books:
  *Nothing But the Truth: A Documentary
      Novel.* Avi
  *The Wright Brothers: How They Invented
      the Airplane.* Russell Freedman

1993-*Missing May*
  by Cynthia Rylant
      Honor Books:
  What Hearts. Bruce Brooks
  *The Dark Thirty: Southern Tales of the
      Supernatural.* Patricia McKissack
  Somewhere in the Darkness. Walter Dean
      Myers

1994- _____

_____

_____

_____

_____

1995- _____

_____

_____

_____

_____

1996- _____

_____

_____

_____

1997- _____

_____

_____

_____

THE POEM

Poetry does not have to be mysterious or difficult writing to understand. It is simply another way to share thoughts and feelings. Why does a writer write poetry? To tell you something. To show you something. What does your friend tell you? What is the message? This is called theme.

What type of person is your friend? Is he friendly? Honest? Loyal? Reliable? Can you trust this person? This is called character.

What does your friend look like? Is he tall? Short? Thin? Fat? Dark hair? Large eyes? Small nose? Big ears? This is description.

How does he talk with you? Is he happy in his words? Is he nervous? Is he sad? How does he feel when he is talking to you? This is called attitude. What is the feeling of your conversation with him? This is tone.

What does he say to you? What are his feelings about what is being said in the conversation? This is his point of view.

These are the things you will find in a poem. Character, theme, description, tone, and point of view are parts of a poem. Just like they are part of your conversation with your friend. Remember that the next time you read a poem.

How do you read a poem? Is there a special formula for reading a poem? A poem should be read several times. Why? Well, you are reading the poem each time for very different reasons. First, read the poem from beginning to end. Don't stop if you are uncertain of a word or a line. Just read. In this way you can get an overview of what the poem is about. Write down any words that you are uncertain of or that are strange to you. Now you are ready for the second reading.

Read each line or part of the poem to see if you understand the language. What is the basic thought that the words present? What is the poem telling you? The message could be as simple as "I like baseball." Now you are ready for a third reading.

Now read the poem again. How does it make you feel? Does the poem present to you a happy feeling? A sad feeling? A confused feeling? Each poem has its own way of looking at the world. Each one is different. Will the student next to you read the poem in the same way that you do? No. Each person is different. And each person will bring different thoughts and feelings to the poem.

POETRY—DEVICES

When writing poetry, poets often use *literary devices*. A device is something used for a purpose—something used to have a particular effect on the reader while reading the poem.* In literary terms, a device can be thought of as a decorative form of wording that the writer uses to make the poem more meaningful, or beautiful, depending on the poem.

Here are some devices to think about as you are reading poems and writing them yourself.

Literal vs. Figurative speech   Symbolism
Imagery   Personification
Simile & Metaphor   Onomatopoeia & Alliteration

Although you may be familiar with some of these terms already, let's go over each device separately and look at some examples so that you can try out these "tools" that authors and poets use in your favorite stories and poems.

Literal vs. Figurative Speech

If your brother tells you "I'm so hungry I could eat a horse," you don't really believe he could eat a horse, do you? This type of language is called *figurative speech*. When people say something that you know is untrue, but is being said to make a point, you say they are making a "figure of speech." Authors may often have characters that use figurative language to make a story more interesting.

If, however, your brother says "I'm hungry," he is speaking literally—he is saying *exactly* what he means. Many people confuse "literal" and "figurative" speech when they say "I literally died!" If they would have literally died—they'd be dead. It would be more correct to say "I figuratively died."

Imagery

Once you understand figurative language, you will be able to understand imagery as well. Imagery comes from the root word "image," which means "picture"—something you can *see*. When you write using the device of imagery, you write so vividly, or creatively, that readers have an image in their mind of what you are saying. Read the following sentence:

Her hair was as black as coal, her eyes blazed like fire.

This sentence uses imagery to give you a picture in your mind of what the woman looks like.

* Literary devices can also be used in other forms of writing, such as stories, novels, and plays.

Simile & Metaphor

When writing figuratively and using imagery as a literary device, similes and metaphors make it possible to "carry out" the imagery and allow the writer's word images to be created. Recall the sentence from the previous example:

Her hair was as black as coal, her eyes blazed like fire.

This sentence is a simile because it uses the words "as" and "like"—these two words make the sentence a simile. "Simile" has the same root as "similar." This may help you remember what a simile is. (Her hair was *similar* to coal, her eyes blazed *similar* to fire.)

If this same sentence was a metaphor, it would read:

Her hair was coal, her eyes blazed fire.

Metaphors *do not* use "as" or like," but instead make a direct comparison. Here is another metaphorical sentence:

The fog *was* a gray blanket that lay over the town.

(If the sentence read "The fog was like a gray blanket that lay over the town," it would be a simile.) "Metaphor" comes from the root "meta" which means change or transformation—in a metaphor words change into other things in order to form a more vivid picture in your mind.

Symbolism

Can you think of some symbols for things? The bald eagle is a symbol. Red is a color that is many times symbolic of blood. How about a heart? A cross? The skull and crossbones pictured on poisonous products? Writer's often use symbolism as a device to get an idea across to the reader. Look at the following:

Leaving the bright daylight of the May afternoon, he entered the gloomy darkness of his old grandmother's house.

In this sentence "light" might symbolize understanding and comfort; the "darkness" might symbolize fright and confusion. Light and dark are often used to symbolize the difference between knowledge and ignorance (or confusion).

Keep in mind that writers do not *always* write symbolically—a writer could talk about night and day without using them as symbols, or use the color red without symbolizing blood. Try to be aware, however, when a writer may be using a symbol to convey a message.

Personification

Personification is exactly what it sounds like—making an *inanimate* object (not living) or animal become like a person by giving the object or animal human qualities:

Dressed in its very best, glowing from head to toe, and standing perfectly straight and tall in our living room, our Christmas tree awaited the flood of admiring relatives on Christmas Eve.

If you think about it hard enough, you can personify anything—even Christmas trees.

Onomatopoeia & Alliteration

Both of these devices are used to "decorate" a poem with sound qualities. By writing or arranging words in a certain way, the author makes words and phrases sound appealing to the reader's (or listener's) ear.

Onomatopoeia is a term for words that sound like their name. Many times onomatopoeias are nonsense words.

buzz (like a bee)   varoom (like a car)   gurgle (like a fish)
plink, plink, plink, (like water in a birdbath)
hiss (like a snake)   pitter patter (like footsteps)

Alliteration is a sound device too. Writers use alliteration when they start many words in the same sentence with the same letter.

Shining sun shone down on Susan as she sowed her sapling seed.

Perhaps the most famous use of alliteration is found in this well-known tongue twister:

Peter Piper picked a peck of pickled peppers. If Peter Piper picked a peck of pickled peppers, how many pickled peppers did Peter Piper pick?

POETRY DEVICES—MATCHING

A. An object that is not alive.

B. Words that sound like the noise they make.

C. Saying exactly what you mean.

D. Using words that convey a vivid picture in your mind's eye.

E. A tool that an author uses to decorate the wording of a poem, story, novel, or play; wording that intensifies the meaning.

F. A comparison using "as" or "like."

G. A *direct* comparison between two things.

H. Using words that are always associated with a specific idea.

I. Using words that describe an inanimate object or animal as a human being.

J. Saying something so exaggerated that it could *never* be true.

K. Using several words in a sentence that begin with the same letter.

1. ____ figurative speech

2. ____ symbolism

3. ____ imagery

4. ____ metaphor

5. ____ alliteration

6. ____ inanimate

7. ____ personification

8. ____ literary device

9. ____ literal speech

10. ____ simile

11. ____ onomatopoeia

SCIENCE FICTION, SCIENCE FACT?

Although science fiction is a type of fantasy, most fantasies are not classified as science fiction. The science fiction story is a special type of fantasy that has several characteristics that make it different from common fantasy stories.

Unlike a typical fantasy in which the plot is controlled by *magical* happenings, a science fiction plot is based on a world controlled by *scientific development and technology*. In story format, science fiction experiments with putting the world we know under a different set of conditions.

Many common elements of the science fiction story include predicting the future, living on other planets, planet settlements and exploration, alien life, space wars, and futuristic technology.

Perhaps the most fascinating characteristic of science fiction is futuristic technology. Did you know that charge cards, lasers, news broadcasts, robots, spacesuits, tape recorders, television, and test-tube babies were all used in science fiction *before* they were invented in real life?

Science fiction writers love to predict the future. Although many things you read about in science fiction seem impossible (time travel, interplanetary travel, etc.), people of long ago thought the same of spacesuits and television—they did not think that these things would ever be invented, but they were—years, sometimes hundreds of years later.

So the next time you read a science fiction story, especially one that was written long ago, be on the lookout for examples of "futuristic technology." The science fiction you are reading may have become science fact!

Here are some places you can write to if you would like more information about science fiction.

Los Angeles Science Fantasy Society
11513 Burbank Boulevard
North Hollywood, CA 91601

Baltimore Science Fiction Society, Inc.
P.O. Box 686
Baltimore, MD 21203

(In your letter, include your age and what you would like information on.)

ROBOTS OF THE FUTURE

Design a robot below. Then describe its capabilities. (You may want to label the different functions of your robot.)

CAPABILITIES:

_____

_____

_____

SPACE CITY OF THE FUTURE

Design a space city of the future below.

What is its name? _____ Where is it located? _____
Label the parts of your city.

TALL TALES

Tall tales are a special kind of folk literature. Tall tales are *American folklore*.

Tall tales began being told early in United States history. When the first settlers came to this country and began moving west they found themselves faced with seemingly impossible tasks. The huge job of clearing the land to build homes, cities, and railroads gave the workers a chance to invent stories about their surroundings and "larger-than-life" people, who like the storytellers themselves, felt *nothing* was impossible.

The stories that arose from this feeling of America's bigness were not only common in the lumbering and railroad towns of the West—they were told in every part of the country and described many types of work.

When discussing and reading tall tales, keep in mind that some of these legendary heroes were real people. They were talked about because they did extraordinary work at their jobs. As other workers related the incredible effort that these "heroes" showed while working, the stories grew, and grew, and grew until the real live people were no longer human, but fictitious super-beings. For this reason, such stories are called "tall tales."

Perhaps the best example of a tall tale that grew from a real man's life is Davy Crockett. Davy Crockett was a backwoodsman who lived in the mountains of Tennessee. He cleared the land, built homesteads, ran for Congress, and died while fighting at the Alamo in 1836. These things really did happen, but as the story goes, "An extraordinary event once occurred in the land of Tennessee. A comet shot out of the sky like a ball of fire. But when the comet hit the top of a mountain, a baby boy tumbled off and landed upright on his feet. His name was Davy Crockett."* The story continues to quickly "grow" from this point on.

Here is a list of other American tall tale heroes (and heroines):

Johnny Appleseed	Paul Bunyan	Joe Magarac
Pecos Bill	Febolb Feboldson	Mose
Jim Bridger	John Henry	Stormalong
Strap Buckner	Casey Jones	Sally Ann Thunder Ann Whirlwind

Use this list for the activities on the following pages. Many book of tall tales include historical information on each character in the stories. The encyclopedia may also have entries on the many legendary American heroes.

* From *American Tall Tales* by Mary Pope Osborne.

NAME _____

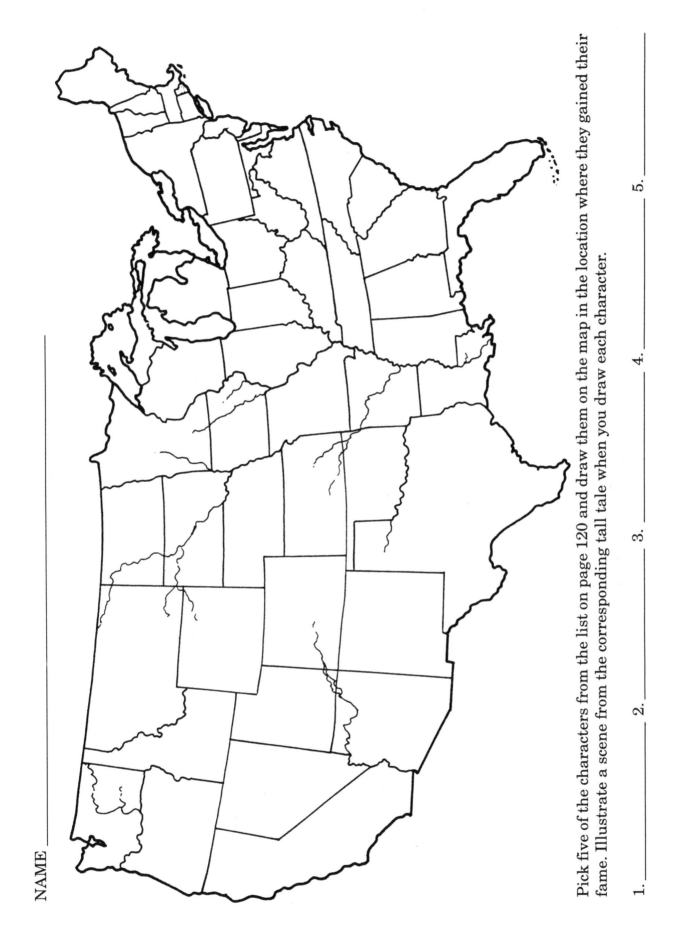

Pick five of the characters from the list on page 120 and draw them on the map in the location where they gained their fame. Illustrate a scene from the corresponding tall tale when you draw each character.

1. _____ 2. _____ 3. _____ 4. _____ 5. _____

TALL TALE ACTIVITIES

1. Pick 5–10 tall tale characters and place them on a time line showing each character's beginnings in American history.

2. Think of a "tall tale" that a friend, parent, grandparent, or other relative has told you. Recount it briefly in a paragraph. Illustrate your tale.

   or

   Think of a famous person from today's times that would make a good character in a tall tale. Write a modern-day tall tale about the person you choose.

3. From the list on page 120, choose three characters and research them in the library. For each hero, explain if the character grew from a real person's life story, or if he/she was totally imaginary. Then tell about the tall tale in your own words.

4. Make a *real* tall tale. Using sheets of 8 1/2" x 11" paper, illustrate the scenes from your favorite tall tale. (Draw the pictures vertically on the paper.) When you are finished, tape the sheets in order and hang your creation high up on a wall (ceiling if necessary) to display your "tall tale."

SUGGESTED AUTHORS FOR GRADE FIVE

ANIMAL STORIES
Howe, James
Lawson, Robert
Moore, Lillian
Pinkwater, D. Manus

CLASSICS
Raintree Short Classics Series

FANTASY
Lewis, C.L.

FICTION
Blume, Judy
Cleary, Beverly
Haywood, Carolyn
Fleischman, Sid

HISTORICAL FICTION
Bulla, Clyde Robert
Disney's American Frontier Series
Fleischman, Paul
Paterson, Katerine
Wilder, Laura Ingalls

HUMOR
Atwater, Richard and Florence
Dana, Barbara
Gilson, Jamie
Lindgren, Astrid
Lowry, Lois

MYSTERY
Dixon, Franklin
Keene, Carolyn
Warner, Gertrude

SCIENCE FICTION
Abels, Harriette
Cameron, Eleanor

THE GLOSSARY

1. *author card*—catalog card which is alphabetized by the author's last name.

2. *appendix*—any materials the author wishes to add to the body of the book such as tables or lists of information. It is found at the back of the book.

3. *bibliography*—an alphabetized list of books which gives the following information: author's name, book title, place, and date of publication and of publisher.

4. *body of book*—the main part of the book.

5. *book index*—an alphabetized list of topics/subjects that can be found in the book.

6. *divided catalog*—a card catalog divided into three sections: author, title, subject.

7. *card catalog*—a collection of cards arranged alphabetically by the author, title, subject.

8. *character*—the animal, person, or nonhuman object in a story, play, poem or short story.

9. *climax*—highest point of tension in a story.

10. *copyright page*—found at the front of the book. It gives book title, author, publisher, place of publication, and copyright date.

11. *conclusion*—the end of the story, play, or short story.

12. *Dewey Decimal System*—system created by Melvil Dewey which arranges nonfiction books according to ten major divisions.

13. *dialogue*—conversations in a play, novel, or short story.

14. *encyclopedia cross reference*—found at the end of an article. It suggests other subjects to check under for additional information.

15. *encyclopedia guide words*—found at the top of the page. Topics are found alphabetically between these words used as guides.

16. *encyclopedia headings*—found within an encyclopedia article. Acts like title headings for information in the article.

17. *encyclopedia index*—alphabetized list of subjects found in the encyclopedia.

18. *encyclopedia key words*—words under which you would most likely find information.

19. *encyclopedia see also references*—found at the end of an article. These subjects are additional subjects under which you can find information.

20. *entry*—information given under a word. Entries are in alphabetical order.

21. *fable*—short, simple story which usually contains a moral or lesson.

22. *fairy tale*—simple story that has a hero, a problem and a happy ending.

23. *falling action*—story events leading to the ending.

24. *fantasy*—story that creates an imaginary world.

25. *fiction*—story which is not real.

26. *glossary*—a mini-dictionary of terms used in the book. It is found at the back of the book.

27. *guide letters*—letters placed on the outside of the catalog drawers that tell what cards are in the drawer.

28. *index*—an alphabetized list of topics/subjects that can be found in the book.

29. *media card*—catalog card used for vertical file, pamphlets, records, slides, or pictures.

30. *nonfiction*—story which is true.

31. *play*—story told by characters in dialogue.

32. *myth*—story which tells the trials and successes of a hero. It usually is a story created by people to explain something in life. Example: why it rains or snows.

33. *point of view*—the author's attitude toward the subject.

34. *preface*—a few words found at the beginning of a book (not all books have them) that explains ideas of the author such as why he wrote the book.

35. **science fiction**—fantasy story usually dealing with another time, another place, and often other beings. Definite rules do exist within the framework of this created world.

36. **subject card**—catalog card which is alphabetized by the subject of the book.

37. **table of contents**—listing of chapter titles found in the beginning of the book.

38. **theme**—major idea of the story, short story, or play.

39. **title card**—catalog card which is alphabetized by the title of the book.

40. **tone**—the "feeling" of the written word, story, play, or poem.

41. **vertical file**—a collection of small items too small to be placed on the library shelves. These may include pamphlets, newspaper clippings, pictures, posters.

NOTES

NOTES